EXTRA-ILLUSTRATED EDITION

∵

VOLUME 34
THE CHRONICLES
OF AMERICA SERIES
ALLEN JOHNSON
EDITOR

GERHARD R. LOMER
CHARLES W. JEFFERYS
ASSISTANT EDITORS

WALT WHITMAN

THE AMERICAN
SPIRIT IN LITERATURE

A CHRONICLE OF
GREAT INTERPRETERS
BY BLISS PERRY

NEW HAVEN: YALE UNIVERSITY PRESS
TORONTO: GLASGOW, BROOK & CO.
LONDON: HUMPHREY MILFORD
OXFORD UNIVERSITY PRESS

1920

105262

CONTENTS

ILLUSTRATIONS

ix

THE AMERICAN SPIRIT IN LITERATURE

∴

CHAPTER I

THE PIONEERS

THE United States of America has been from the beginning in a perpetual change. The physical and mental restlessness of the American and the temporary nature of many of his arrangements are large   to the experimental character of the exploration and development of this continent. The new energies released by the settlement of the colonies were indeed guided by stern determination, wise forethought, and inventive skill; but no one has ever really known the outcome of the experiment. It is a story of faith, of

> Effort, and expectation, and desire,
> And something evermore about to be.

An Alexander Hamilton may urge with passionate force the adoption of the Constitution, without any firm conviction as to its permanence. The most clear-sighted American of the Civil War period recognized this element of uncertainty in our American adventure when he declared: "We are now testing whether this nation, or any nation so conceived and so dedicated, can long endure." More than fifty years have passed since that war reaffirmed the binding force of the Constitution and apparently sealed the perpetuity of the Union. Yet the gigantic economic and social changes now in progress are serving to show that the United States has its full share of the anxieties which beset all human institutions in this daily altering world.

"We are but strangers in an inn, but passengers in a ship," said Roger Williams. This sense of the transiency of human effort, the perishable nature of human institutions, was quick in the consciousness of the gentleman adventurers and sober Puritan citizens who emigrated from England to the New World. It had been a familiar note in the poetry of that Elizabethan period which had followed with such breathless interest the exploration of America. It was a conception which could be shared alike by a saint like John Cotton or a soldier of fortune like John Smith. Men are tent-dwellers. Today they settle here, and tomorrow they have struck camp and are gone. We are strangers and sojourners, as all our fathers were.

This instinct of the camper has stamped itself upon American life and thought. Venturesomeness, physical and moral daring, resourcefulness in emergencies, indifference to negligible details, wastefulness of materials, boundless hope and confidence in the morrow, are characteristics of the American. It is scarcely an exaggeration to say that the "good American" has been he who has most resembled a good camper. He has had robust health — unless or until he has abused it, — a tolerant disposition, and an ability to apply his fingers or his brain to many unrelated and unexpected tasks. He is disposed to blaze his own trail. He has a touch of prodigality, and, withal, a knack of keeping his tent or his affairs in better order than they seem. Above all, he has been ever ready to break camp when he feels the impulse to wander. He likes to be "foot-loose." If he does not build his roads as solidly as the Roman roads were built, nor his houses like the English houses, it is because he feels that he is here today and gone tomorrow. If he has squandered the physical resources of his neighborhood, cutting the forests recklessly, exhausting the soil, surrendering water power and minerals into a few far-clutching fingers, he has done it because he expects, like Voltaire's Signor Pococurante, "to have a new garden tomorrow, built on a nobler plan." When New York State grew too crowded for Cooper's Leather-Stocking, he shouldered his pack, whistled to his dog, glanced at the sun, and struck a bee-line for the Mississippi. Nothing could be more typical of the first three hundred years of American history.

The traits of the pioneer have thus been the characteristic traits of the American in action. The memories of successive generations have tended to stress these qualities to the neglect of others. Everyone who has enjoyed the free life of the woods will confess that his own judgment upon his casual summer associates turns, quite naturally and almost exclusively, upon their characteristics as woodsmen. Out of the woods, these gentlemen may be more or less admirable divines, pedants, men of affairs; but the verdict of their companions in the forest is based chiefly upon the single question of their adaptability to the environment of the camp. Are they quick of eye and foot, skillful with rod and gun, cheerful on rainy days, ready to do a little more than their share of drudgery? If so, memory holds them.

Some such unconscious selection as this has been at work in the classification of our representative men. The building of the nation and the literary expression of its purpose and ideals are tasks which have called forth the strength of a great variety of individuals. Some of these men have proved to be peculiarly fitted for a specific service, irrespective of the question of their general intellectual powers, or their rank as judged by the standard of European performance in the same field. Thus the battle of New Orleans, in European eyes a mere bit of frontier fighting, made Andrew Jackson a "hero" as indubitably as if he had defeated Napoleon at Waterloo. It gave him the Presidency.

The analogy holds in literature. Certain expressions of American sentiment or conviction have served to summarize or to clarify the spirit of the nation. The authors of these productions have frequently won the recognition and affection of their contemporaries by means of prose and verse quite unsuited to sustain the test of severe critical standards. Neither Longfellow's *Excelsior* nor Poe's *Bells* nor Whittier's *Maud Muller* is among the best poems of the three writers in question, yet there was something in each of these productions which caught the fancy of a whole American generation. It expressed one phase of the national mind in a given historical period.

The historian of literature is bound to take account of this question of literary vogue, as it is highly significant of the temper of successive generations in any country. But it is of peculiar interest to the student of the literature produced in the United States. Is this literature "American," or is it "English literature in America," as Professor Wendell and other scholars have preferred to call it? I should be one of the last to minimize the enormous influence of England upon the mind and the writing of all the English-speaking countries of the globe.   Yet it will be one of the purposes of the present book to indicate the existence here, even in colonial times, of a point of view differing from that of the mother country, and destined to differ increasingly with the lapse of time. Since the formation of our Federal Union, in particular, the books produced in the United States have tended to exhibit certain characteristics which differentiate them from the books produced in other English-speaking countries. We must beware, of course, of what the late Charles Francis Adams once called the "filiopietistic" fallacy. The "American" qualities of our literature must be judged in connection with its conformity to universal standards of excellence. Tested by any universal standard, *The Scarlet Letter* is a notable romance. It has won a secure place among the literature written by men of English blood and speech. Yet to overlook the peculiarly local or provincial characteristics of this remarkable story is to miss the secret of its inspiration. It could have been written only by a New Englander, in the atmosphere of a certain epoch.

Our task, then, in this rapid review of the chief interpreters of the American spirit in literature, is a twofold one. We are primarily concerned with a procession of men, each of whom is interesting as an individual and as a writer. But we cannot watch the individuals long without perceiving the general direction of their march, the ideas that animate them, the common hopes and loyalties that make up the life of their spirit. To become aware of these general tendencies is to understand the "American" note in our national writing.

Our historians have taught us that the history of the United States is an evolution towards political unity.   The separatist, particularist movements are gradually thrust to one side.   In literary history, likewise, we best remember those authors who fall into line with what we now perceive to have been the course of our literary development.   The erratic men and women, the "sports" of the great experiment, are ultimately neglected by the critics, unless, like the leaders of political insurrections, those writing men and women have raised a notable standard of revolt.   No doubt the apparently unique literary specimens, if clearly understood in their origins and surroundings, would be found rooted in the general laws of literary evolution.   But these laws are not easy to codify and we must avoid the temptation to discover, in any particular period, more of unity than there actually was.   And we must always remember that there will be beautiful prose and verse unrelated to the main national tendencies save as "the literature of escape."   We owe this lesson to the genius of Edgar Allan Poe.

Let us test these principles by applying them to the earliest colonists.   The first book written on the soil of what is now the United States was Captain John Smith's *True Relation* of the planting of the Virginia colony in 1607.   It was published in

London in 1608. The Captain was a typical Elizabethan adventurer, with a gift, like so many of his class, for picturesque narrative. In what sense, if at all, may his writings on American topics be classified as "American" literary productions? It is clear that his experiences in the New World were only one phase of the variegated life of this English soldier of fortune. But the American imagination has persistently claimed him as representing something peculiarly ours, namely, a kind of pioneer hardihood, resourcefulness, leadership, which was essential to the exploration and conquest of the wilderness. Most of Smith's companions were unfitted for the ordeal which he survived. They perished miserably in the "starving time." But he was of the stuff from which triumphant immigrants have ever been made, and it is our recognition of the presence of these qualities in the Captain which makes us think of his books dealing with America as if they were "American books." There are other narratives by colonists temporarily residing in the Virginia plantations which gratify our historical curiosity, but which we no more consider a part of American literature than the books written by Stevenson, Kipling, and Wells during their casual visits to this country.

But Captain Smith's *True Relation* impresses us, like Mark Twain's *Roughing It*, with being somehow true to type. In each of these books the possible unveracities in detail are a confirmation of their representative American character.

In other words, we have unconsciously formulated, in the course of centuries, a general concept of "the pioneer." Novelists, poets, and historians have elaborated this conception. Nothing is more inevitable than our reaching back to the beginning of the seventeenth century and endeavoring to select, among the thousands of Englishmen who emigrated or even thought of emigrating to this country, those who possessed the genuine heart and sinew of the permanent settler.

Oliver Cromwell, for instance, is said to have thought of emigrating hither in 1637. If he had joined his friends John Cotton and Roger Williams in New England, who can doubt that the personal characteristics of "my brave Oliver" would today be identified with the "American" qualities which we discover in 1637 on the shores of Massachusetts Bay? And what an American settler Cromwell would have made!

If we turn from physical and moral daring to the

field of theological and political speculation, it is easy today to select, among the writings of the earliest colonists, certain radical utterances which seem to presage the very temper of the late eighteenth century. Pastor John Robinson's farewell address to the Pilgrims at Leyden in 1620 contained the famous words: "The Lord has more truth yet to break forth out of His holy Word. I cannot sufficiently bewail the condition of the reformed churches, who are come to a period in religion. . . . Luther and Calvin were great and shining lights in their times, yet they penetrated not into the whole counsel of God." Now John Robinson, like Oliver Cromwell, never set foot on American soil, but he is identified, none the less, with the spirit of American liberalism in religion.

In political discussion, the early emergence of that type of independence familiar to the decade 1765–75 is equally striking. In a letter written in 1818, John Adams insisted that "the principles and feelings which produced the Revolution ought to be traced back for two hundred years, and sought in the history of the country from the first plantations in America." "I have always laughed," he declared in an earlier letter, "at the affectation of representing American independence as a novel idea, as a modern discovery, as a late invention. The idea of it as a possible thing, as a probable event, nay as a necessary and unavoidable measure, in case Great Britain should assume an unconstitutional authority over us, has been familiar to Americans from the first settlement of the country."

There is, then, a predisposition, a latent or potential Americanism which existed long before the United States came into being. Now that our political unity has become a fact, the predisposition is certain to be regarded by our own and by future generations as evidence of a state of mind which made our separate national life inevitable. Yet to Thomas Hutchinson, a sound historian and honest man, the last Royal Governor of Massachusetts, a separate national life seemed in 1770 an unspeakable error and calamity.

The seventeenth-century colonists were predominantly English, in blood, in traditions, and in impulses. Whether we look at Virginia or Plymouth or at the other colonies that were planted in swift succession along the seaboard, it is clear that we are dealing primarily with men of the English race. Most of them would have declared, with as much emphasis as Francis Hopkinson a

century later, "We of America are in all respects
Englishmen." Professor Edward Channing thinks
that it took a century of exposure to colonial conditions to force the English in America away from
the traditions and ideals of those who continued
to live in the old land. But the student of literature must keep constantly in mind that these
English colonizers represented no single type of the
national character. There were many men of
many minds even within the contracted cabin of
the *Mayflower*. The "sifted wheat" was by no
means all of the same variety.

For Old England was never more torn by diver-
gent thought and subversive act than in the period
between the death of Elizabeth in 1603 and the
Revolution of 1688. In this distracted time who
could say what was really "English"? Was it
James the First or Raleigh? Archbishop Laud or
John Cotton? Charles the First or Cromwell?
Charles the Second or William Penn? Was it
Churchman, Presbyterian, Independent, Separatist, Quaker? One is tempted to say that the
title of Ben Jonson's comedy *Every Man in his
Humour* became the standard of action for two
whole generations of Englishmen, and that there is
no common denominator for emigrants of such

varied pattern as Smith and Sandys of Virginia, Morton of Merrymount, John Winthrop, "Sir" Christopher Gardiner and Anne Hutchinson of Boston, and Roger Williams of Providence. They seem as miscellaneous as "Kitchener's Army."

It is true that we can make certain distinctions. Virginia, as has often been said, was more like a continuation of English society, while New England represented a digression from English society. There were then, as now, "stand-patters" and "progressives." It was the second class who, while retaining very conservative notions about property, developed a fearless intellectual radicalism which has written itself into the history of the United States. But to the student of early American literature all such generalizations are of limited value. He is dealing with individual men, not with "Cavalier" or "Roundhead" as such. He has learned from recent historians to distrust any such facile classification of the first colonists. He knows by this time that there were aristocrats in Massachusetts and commoners in Virginia; that the Pilgrims of Plymouth were more tolerant than the Puritans of Boston, and that Rhode Island was more tolerant than either. Yet useful as these general statements may be, the interpreter of men of letters must always go back of the racial type or the social system to the individual person. He recognizes, as a truth for him, that theory of creative evolution which holds that in the ascending progress of the race each thinking person becomes a species by himself.

While something is gained, then, by remembering that the racial instincts and traditions of the first colonists were overwhelmingly English, and that their political and ethical views were the product of a turbulent and distraught time, it is even more important to note how the physical situation of the colonists affected their intellectual and moral, as well as their political problems. Among the emigrants from England, as we have seen, there were great varieties of social status, religious opinion, individual motive. But at least they all possessed the physical courage and moral hardihood to risk the dangerous voyage, the fearful hardships, and the vast uncertainties of the new life. To go out at all, under the pressure of any motive, was to meet triumphantly a searching test. It was in truth a "sifting," and though a few picturesque rascals had the courage to go into exile while a few saints may have been deterred, it is a truism to say that the pioneers were made up of brave men and braver women.

It cannot be asserted that their courage was the result of any single, dominating motive, equally operative in all of the colonies. Mrs. Hemans's familiar line about seeking "freedom to worship God" was measurably true of the Pilgrims of Plymouth, about whom she was writing. But the far more important Puritan emigration to Massachusetts under Winthrop aimed not so much at "freedom" as at the establishment of a theocracy according to the Scriptures. These men straightway denied freedom of worship, not only to newcomers who sought to join them, but to those members of their own company who developed independent ways of thinking. The list of motives for emigration ran the whole gamut, from missionary fervor for converting the savages, down through a commendable desire for gain, to the perhaps no less praiseworthy wish to escape a debtor's prison or the pillory. A few of the colonists were rich. Some were beggars or indentured servants. Most of them belonged to the middle class. John Harvard was the son of a butcher; Thomas Shepard, the son of a grocer; Roger Williams, the son of a tailor. But all three were university bred and were natural leaders of men.

Once arrived in the wilderness, the pioneer life common to all of the colonists began instantly to exert its slow, irresistible pressure upon their minds and to mould them into certain ways of thinking and feeling. Without some perception of these modes of thought and emotion a knowledge of the spirit of our literature is impossible. Take, for instance, the mere physical situation of the first colonists, encamped on the very beach of the wide ocean with an illimitable forest in their rear. Their provisions were scanty. They grew watchful of the strange soil, of the new skies, of the unknown climate. Even upon the voyage over, John Winthrop thought that "the declination of the pole star was much, even to the view, beneath that it is in England," and that "the new moon, when it first appeared, was much smaller than at any time he had seen it in England." Here was a man evidently using his eyes with a new interest in natural phenomena. Under these changed skies the mind began gradually to change also.

At first the colonists felt themselves an outpost of Europe, a forlorn hope of the Protestant Reformation. "We shall be as a city upon a hill," said

2

Winthrop. "The eyes of all people are upon us." Their creed was Calvinism, then in its third generation of dominion and a European doctrine which was not merely theological but social and political. The emigrant Englishmen were soon to discover that it contained a doctrine of human rights based upon human needs. At the beginning of their novel experience they were doubtless unaware of any alteration in their theories. But they were facing a new situation, and that new situation became an immense factor in their unconscious growth. Their intellectual and moral problems shifted, as a boat shifts her ballast when the wind blows from a new quarter. The John Cotton preaching in a shed in the new Boston had come to "suffer a sea-change" from the John Cotton who had been rector of St. Botolph's splendid church in Lincolnshire. The "church without a bishop" and the "state without a king" became a different church and state from the old, however loyally the ancient forms and phrases were retained.

If the political problems of equality which were latent in Calvinism now began to take on a different meaning under the democratic conditions of pioneer life, the inner, spiritual problems of that amazing creed were intensified. "Fallen" human nature remained the same, whether in the crowded cosmopolitan streets of Holland and London, or upon the desolate shores of Cape Cod. But the moral strain of the old insoluble conflict between "fixed fate" and "free will" was heightened by the physical loneliness of the colonists. Each soul must fight its own unaided, unending battle. In that moral solitude, as in the physical solitude of the settlers upon the far northwestern prairies of a later epoch, many a mind snapped. Unnatural tension was succeeded by unnatural crimes. But for the stronger intellects New England Calvinism became a potent spiritual gymnastic, where, as in the Swedish system of bodily training, one lifts imaginary and ever-increasing weights with imaginary and ever-increasing effort, flexor and extensor muscles pulling against one another, driven by the will. Calvinism bred athletes as well as maniacs.

The new situation, again, turned many of the theoretical speculations of the colonists into practical issues. Here, for example, was the Indian. Was he truly a child of God, possessing a soul, and, if so, had he partaken of the sin of Adam? These questions perplexed the saintly Eliot and the generous Roger Williams. But before many years the query as to whether a Pequot warrior had a soul became suddenly less important than the practical question as to whether the Pequot should be allowed any further chances of taking the white man's scalp. On this last issue the colonists were unanimous in the negative.

It would be easy to multiply such instances of a gradual change of view. But beneath all the changes and all the varieties of individual behavior in the various colonies that began to dot the seaboard, certain qualities demanded by the new surroundings are felt in colonial life and in colonial writings. One of these is the instinct for order, or at least that degree of order essential to the existence of a camp. It was not in vain that John Smith sought to correct the early laxness at Jamestown by the stern edict: "He that will not work, neither shall he eat." Dutch and Quaker colonies taught the same inexorable maxim of thrift. Soon there was work enough for all, at good wages, but the lesson had been taught. It gave Franklin's *Poor Richard* mottoes their flavor of homely, experienced truth.

Order in daily life led straight to political order, just as the equality and resourcefulness of the frontier, stimulated by isolation from Europe, led to political independence. The pioneer learned to make things for himself instead of sending to London for them, and by and by he grew as impatient of waiting for a political edict from London as he would become in waiting for a London plough. "This year," wrote one colonist, "ye will go to complain to the Parliament, and the next year they will send to see how it is, and the third year the government is changed." The time was coming when no more complaints would be sent.

One of the most startling instances of this colonial instinct for self-government is the case of Thomas Hooker. Trained in Emmanuel College of the old Cambridge, he arrived in the new Cambridge in 1633. He grew restless under its theocratic government, being, it was said, "a person who when he was doing his Master's work would put a king into his pocket." So he led the famous migration of 1636 from Massachusetts to Hartford, and there helped to create a federation of independent towns which made their own constitution without mentioning any king, and became one of the corner-stones of American democracy. In May, 1638, Hooker declared in a sermon before the General Court "that the choice of public magistrates belongs unto the people by God's own allowance," and "that they who have the power to appoint officers and magistrates, it is in their power, also, to set the bounds and limitations of the power and place into which they call them." The reason of this is: "*Because the foundation of authority is laid, firstly, in the free consent of the people.*" This high discourse antedates the famous pamphlets on liberty by Milton. It is a half-century earlier than Locke's *Treatise on Government*, a century and a quarter earlier than Rousseau's *Contrat Social*, and it precedes by one hundred and thirty-eight years the American Declaration of Independence.

But the slightest acquaintance with colonial writings will reveal the fact that such political radicalism as Thomas Hooker's was accompanied by an equally striking conservatism in other directions. One of these conservative traits was the pioneer's respect for property, and particularly for the land cleared by his own toil. Gladstone once spoke of possession of the soil as the most important and most operative of all social facts. Free-footed as the pioneer colonist was, he was disinclined to part with his land without a substantial price for it. The land at his disposal was practically illimitable, but he showed a very

English tenacity in safeguarding his hold upon his own portion.

Very English, likewise, was his attachment to the old country as "home." The lighter and the more serious writings of the colonists are alike in their respect for the past. In the New England settlements, although not at first in Virginia, there was respect for learning and for an educated clergy. The colonists revered the Bible. They maintained a stubborn regard for the Common Law of England. Even amid all the excitement of a successful rebellion from the mother country, this Common Law still held the Americans to the experience of the inescapable past.

Indeed, as the reader of today lifts his eyes from the pages of the books written in America during the seventeenth century, and tries to meditate upon the general difference between them and the English books written during the same period, he will be aware of the firmness with which the conservative forces held on this side of the Atlantic. It was only one hundred years from the Great Armada of 1588 to the flight of James Second, the last of the Stuart Kings. With that Revolution of 1688 the struggles characteristic of the seventeenth century in England came to an end. A new working basis is found for thought, politics, society, literature.   But while those vast changes had been shaking England, two generations of American colonists had cleared their forests, fought the savages, organized their townships and their trade, put money in their purses, and lived, though as yet hardly suspecting it, a life that was beginning to differentiate them from the men of the Old World. We must now glance at the various aspects of this isolated life of theirs, as it is revealed in their books.

CHAPTER II

THE FIRST COLONIAL LITERATURE

THE simplest and oldest group of colonial writings is made up of records of exploration and adventure. They are like the letters written from California in 1849 to the "folks back East." Addressed to home-keeping Englishmen across the sea, they describe the new world, explain the present situation of the colonists, and express their hopes for the future. Captain John Smith's *True Relation*, already alluded to, is the typical production of this class: a swift marching book, full of eager energy, of bluff and breezy picturesqueness, and of triumphant instinct for the main chance. Like most of the Elizabethans, he cannot help poetizing in his prose. Cod-fishing is to him a "sport"; "and what sport doth yeald a more pleasing content, and lesse hurt or charge then angling with a hooke, and crossing the sweete ayre from Isle to Isle, over the silent streams of a calme Sea?" But the gallant Captain is also capable of very plain speech, Cromwellian in its simplicity, as when he writes back to the London stockholders of the Virginia Company: "When you send again, I entreat you rather send but thirty carpenters, husbandmen, gardeners, fishermen, blacksmiths, masons, and diggers up of trees' roots, well provided, than a thousand of such as we have."

America was but an episode in the wide wanderings of Captain Smith, but he owes his place in human memory today to the physical and mental energy with which he met the demands of a new situation, and to the vividness with which he dashed down in words whatever his eyes had seen. Whether, in that agreeable passage about Pocahontas, he was guilty of romancing a little, no one really knows, but the Captain, as the first teller of this peculiarly American type of story, will continue to have an indulgent audience.

But other exiles in Virginia were skillful with the pen. William Strachey's *True Reportory of the Wrack of Sir Thomas Gates, Kt., vpon and from the islands of the Bermudas* may or may not have given a hint to Shakespeare for the storm-scene in *The Tempest*. In either case it is admirable writing, flexible, sensitive, shrewdly observant. Whitaker,

the apostle of Virginia, mingles, like many a missionary of the present day, the style of an exhorter
with a keen discernment of the traits of the savage
mind.   George Percy, fresh from Northumberland,
tells in a language as simple as Defoe's the piteous
tale of five months of illness and starvation,
watched by "those wild and cruel Pagans."   John
Pory, of "the strong potations," who thinks that
"good company is the soul of this life," nevertheless comforts himself in his solitude among the
"crystal rivers and odoriferous woods" by reflecting
that he is escaping envy and expense.   George
Sandys, scholar and poet, finds his solace during
a Virginia exile in continuing his translation of
Ovid's *Metamorphoses*.   Colonel Norwood, an adventurer who belongs to a somewhat later day,
since he speaks of having "read Mr. Smith's
travels," draws the long bow of narrative quite as
powerfully as the redoubtable Smith, and far more
smoothly, as witness his accounts of starvation on
shipboard and cannibalism on shore.   This Colonel
is an artist who would have delighted Stevenson.

All of these early tellers of Virginia tales were
Englishmen, and most of them returned to England, where their books were printed and their
remaining lives were passed.   But far to the north-

east of Virginia there were two colonies of men who earned the right to say, in William Bradford's quiet words, "It is not with us as with other men, whom small things can discourage, or small discontentments cause to wish themselves at home again." One was the colony of Pilgrims at Plymouth, headed by Bradford himself. The other was the Puritan colony of Massachusetts Bay, with John Winthrop as governor.

Bradford and Winthrop have left journals which are more than chronicles of adventure. They record the growth and government of a commonwealth. Both Bradford and Winthrop were natural leaders of men, grave, dignified, solid, endowed with a spirit that bred confidence. Each was learned. Winthrop, a lawyer and man of property, had a higher social standing than Bradford, who was one of the Separatists of Robinson's flock at Leyden. But the Pilgrim of the *Mayflower* and the well-to-do Puritan of the Bay Colony both wrote their annals like gentlemen and scholars. Bradford's *History of Plymouth Plantation* runs from 1620 to 1647. Winthrop's diary, now printed as the *History of New England*, begins with his voyage in 1630 and closes in the year of his death, 1649. As records of an Anglo-Saxon

experiment in self-government under pioneer conditions these books are priceless; as human documents, they illuminate the Puritan character; as
for "literary" value in the narrow sense of that
word, neither Bradford nor Winthrop seems to
have thought of literary effect. Yet the leader of
the Pilgrims has passages of grave sweetness and
charm, and his sketch of his associate, Elder
Brewster, will bear comparison with the best
English biographical writing of that century.
Winthrop is perhaps more varied in tone, as he is
in matter, but he writes throughout as a ruler of
men should write, with "decent plainness and
manly freedom." His best known pages, justly
praised by Tyler and other historians of American
thought, contain his speech before the General
Court in 1645 on the nature of true liberty. No
paragraphs written in America previous to the
Revolution would have given more pleasure to
Abraham Lincoln, but it is to be feared that Lincoln never saw Governor Winthrop's book, though
his own ancestor, Samuel Lincoln of Hingham,
lived under Winthrop's jurisdiction.

The theory of government held by the dominant
party of the first two generations of New England
pioneers has often been called a "theocracy,"

that is to say, a government according to the Word of God as expounded and enforced by the clergy. The experiment was doomed to ultimate failure, for it ran counter to some of the noblest instincts of human nature. But its administration was in the hands of able men. The power of the clergy was well-nigh absolute. The political organization of the township depended upon the ecclesiastical organization as long as the right to vote was confined to church members. How sacrosanct and awful was the position of the clergyman may be perceived from Hawthorne's *The Minister's Black Veil* and *The Scarlet Letter*.

Yet it must be said that men like Hooker and Cotton, Shepard and Norton, had every instinct and capacity for leadership. With the notable exception of Hooker, such men were aristocrats, holding John Winthrop's opinion that "Democracy is, among most civil nations, accounted the meanest and worst form of government." They were fiercely intolerant. The precise reason for the Hooker migration from Cambridge to Hartford in 1636 — the very year of the founding of Harvard — was prudently withheld, but it is now thought to be the instinct of escape from the clerical architects of the Cambridge Platform. Yet no one

would today call Thomas Hooker a liberal in religion, pioneer in political liberty though he proved
to be.   His extant sermons have the steady stroke
of a great hammer, smiting at the mind and heart.
"Others because they have felt the heavy hand
of God . . . upon these grounds they build their
hopes: 'I have had my hell in this life, and I hope
to have heaven in the world to come; I hope the
worst is over.'"   Not so, thunders the preacher
in reply: "Sodom and Gomorrah they burnt in
brimstone and they shall burn in hell."   One of
Hooker's successors has called him "a son of
thunder and a son of consolation by turns."   The
same may be said of Thomas Shepard, another
graduate of Emmanuel College in the old Cambridge, who became the "soul-melting preacher"
of the newer Cambridge by the Charles.   Pure,
ravishing notes of spiritual devotion still sing
themselves in his pages.   He is wholly Calvinist.
He thinks "the truth is a poor mean thing in itself"
and that the human reason cannot be "the last
resolution of all doubts," which must be sought
only in the written Word of God.   He holds it "a
tough work, a wonderful hard matter to be saved."
"Jesus Christ is not got with a wet finger."   Yet,
like so many mystics, he yearns to be "covered

with God, as with a cloud," to be "drowned, plunged, and swallowed up with God." One hundred years later we shall find this same rhapsodic ecstasy in the meditations of Jonathan Edwards.

John Cotton, the third of the mighty men in the early Colonial pulpit, owes his fame more to his social and political influence than to his literary power. Yet even that was thought commanding. Trained, like Hooker and Shepard, at Emmanuel College, and fresh from the rectorship of St. Botolph's in the Lincolnshire Boston, John Cotton dominated that new Boston which was named in his honor. He became the Pope of the theocracy; a clever Pope and not an unkindly one. He seems to have shared some of the opinions of Anne Hutchinson, though he "pronounced the sentence of admonition" against her, says Winthrop, with much zeal and detestation of her errors. Hawthorne, in one of his ironic moods, might have done justice to this scene. Cotton was at heart too liberal for his rôle of Primate, and fate led him to persecute a man whose very name has become a symbol of victorious tolerance, Roger Williams.

Williams, known today as a friend of Cromwell, Milton, and Sir Harry Vane, had been exiled from

Massachusetts for maintaining that the civil power had no jurisdiction over conscience. This doctrine was fatal to the existence of a theocratic state dominated by the church. John Cotton was perfectly logical in "enlarging" Roger Williams into the wilderness, but he showed less than his usual discretion in attacking the quick-tempered Welshman in pamphlets. It was like asking Hotspur if he would kindly consent to fight. Back and forth the books fly, for Williams loves this game. His *Bloody Tenet of Persecution for Cause of Conscience* calls forth Mr. Cotton's *Bloody Tenet washed and made white in the Blood of the Lamb;* and this in turn provokes the torrential flood of Williams's masterpiece, *The Bloody Tenet yet more Bloody, by Mr. Cotton's endeavor to wash it white in the Blood of the Lamb.* There is glorious writing here, and its effect cannot be suggested by quoting sentences. But there is one sentence in a letter written by Williams in his old age to his fellow-townsmen of Providence which points the whole moral of the terrible mistake made by the men who sought spiritual liberty in America for themselves, only to deny that same liberty to others. "I have only one motion and petition," begs this veteran pioneer who had forded many a swollen stream and built many a rude bridge in the Plantations: "it is this, that after you have got over the black brook of some soul bondage yourselves, you tear not down the bridge after you."

It is for such wise and humane counsels as this that Roger Williams is remembered. His opponents had mightier intellects than his, but the world has long since decided against them. Colonial sermon literature is read today chiefly by antiquarians who have no sympathy for the creed which once gave it vitality. Its theology, like the theology of *Paradise Lost* or the *Divine Comedy*, has sunk to the bottom of the black brook. But we cannot judge fairly the contemporary effect of this pulpit literature without remembering the passionate faith that made pulpit and pews copartners in a supreme spiritual struggle. Historians properly insist upon the æsthetic poverty of the New England Puritans; that their rule of life cut them off from an enjoyment of the dramatic literature of their race, then just closing its most splendid epoch; that they had little poetry or music and no architecture and plastic art. But we must never forget that to men of their creed the Sunday sermons and the week-day "lectures" served as oratory, poetry, and drama. These outpourings of the mind and heart of their spiritual leaders were the very stuff of human passion in its intensest forms. Puritan churchgoers, passing hours upon hours every week in rapt absorption with the noblest of all poetry and prose in the pages of their chief book, the Bible, were at least as sensitive to the beauty of words and the sweep of emotions as our contemporaries upon whose book-shelves Spenser and Milton stand unread.

It is only by entering into the psychology of the period that we can estimate its attitude towards the poetry written by the pioneers themselves. The *Bay Psalm Book* (1640), the first book printed in the colonies, is a wretched doggerel arrangement of the magnificent King James Version of the Psalms, designed to be sung in churches. Few of the New England churches could sing more than half-a-dozen tunes, and a pitch-pipe was for a long time the only musical instrument allowed. Judged as hymnology or poetry, the *Bay Psalm Book* provokes a smile. But the men and women who used it as a handbook of devotion sang it with their hearts aflame. In judging such a popular seventeenth-century poem as Wigglesworth's *Day of Doom* one must strip oneself quite free from the twentieth century, and pretend to be sitting in the

chimney-corner of a Puritan kitchen, reading
aloud by that firelight which, as Lowell once
humorously suggested, may have added a "live-
lier relish" to the poet's "premonitions of eternal
combustion." Lowell could afford to laugh about
it, having crossed that particular black brook.
But for several generations the boys and girls of
New England had read the *Day of Doom* as if
Mr. Wigglesworth, the gentle and somewhat
sickly minister of Malden, had veritably peeped
into Hell. It is the present fashion to underestimate the power of Wigglesworth's verse. At
its best it has a trampling, clattering shock like a
charge of cavalry and a sound like clanging steel.
Mr. Kipling and other cunning ballad-makers
have imitated the peculiar rhyme structure chosen
by the nervous little parson. But no living poet
can move his readers to the fascinated horror once
felt by the Puritans as they followed Wigglesworth's relentless gaze into the future of the soul's
destiny.

Historical curiosity may still linger, of course,
over other verse-writers of the period. Anne
Bradstreet's poems, for instance, are not without
grace and womanly sweetness, in spite of their
didactic themes and portentous length. But this

lady, born in England, the daughter of Governor
Dudley and later the wife of Governor Bradstreet,
chose to imitate the more fantastic of the moraliz-
ing poets of England and France.   There is little
in her hundreds of pages which seems today the
inevitable outcome of her own experience in the
New World.   For readers who like roughly mis-
chievous satire, of a type initiated in England by
Bishop Hall and Donne, there is *The Simple
Cobbler of Agawam* written by the roving clergyman Nathaniel Ward.   But he lived only a dozen
years in Massachusetts, and his satirical pictures
are scarcely more "American" than the satire
upon German professors in *Sartor Resartus* is
"German."   Like   Charles   Dickens's   *American
Notes*, Ward's give the reaction of a born English-
man in the presence of the sights and the talk and
the personages of the transatlantic world.

Of all the colonial writings of the seventeenth
century, those that have lost least of their interest
through the lapse of years are narratives of struggles with the Indians.   The image of the "bloody
savage" has always hovered in the background of
the American imagination. Our boys and girls have
"played Indian" from the beginning, and the actual
Indian is still found, as for three hundred years past,

upon the frontier fringe of our civilization. Novelists like Cooper, historians like Parkman, poets like Longfellow, have dealt with the rich material offered by the life of the aborigines, but the long series begins with the scribbled story of colonists. Here are comedy and tragedy, plain narratives of trading and travel, missionary zeal and triumphs; then the inevitable alienation of the two races and the doom of the native.

The "noble savage" note may be found in John Rolfe, the husband of Pocahontas, with whom, poor fellow, his "best thoughts are so intangled and enthralled." Other Virginians, like Smith, Strachey, and Percy, show close naturalistic observation, touched with the abounding Elizabethan zest for novelties. To Alexander Whitaker, however, these "naked slaves of the devil" were "not so simple as some have supposed." He yearned and labored over their souls, as did John Eliot and Roger Williams and Daniel Gookin of New England. In the Pequot War of 1637 the grim settlers resolved to be rid of that tribe once for all, and the narratives of Captain Edward Johnson and Captain John Mason, who led in the storming and slaughter at the Indians' Mystic Fort, are as piously relentless as anything in the Old Testa-

ment.   Cromwell at Drogheda, not long after, had
soldiers no more merciless than these extermina-
ting Puritans, who wished to plough their fields
henceforth in peace.   A generation later the storm
broke again in King Philip's War.   Its tales of
massacre, captivity, and single-handed fighting
linger in the American imagination still.   Typical
pamphlets are Mary Rowlandson's thrilling tale
of the Lancaster massacre and her subsequent
captivity, and the loud-voiced Captain Church's
unvarnished description of King Philip's death.
The King, shot down like a wearied bull-moose in
the deep swamp, "fell upon his face in the mud
and water, with his gun under him."   They
"drew him through the mud to the upland; and
a doleful, great, naked dirty beast he looked like."
The head brought only thirty shillings at Plymouth: "scanty reward and poor encouragement,"
thought Captain Church.   William Hubbard,
the minister of Ipswich, wrote a comprehensive
*Narrative of the Troubles with the Indians in New
England*, bringing the history down to 1677.
Under the better known title of *Indian Wars*, this
fervid and dramatic tale, penned in a quiet parsonage, has stirred the pulses of every succeeding
generation.

The close of King Philip's War, 1676, coinciding as it does with Bacon's Rebellion in Virginia, marks an era in the development of our independent life. The events of that year, in the words of Professor Tyler, "established two very considerable facts, namely, that English colonists in America could be so provoked as to make physical resistance to the authority of England, and, second, that English colonists in America could, in the last resort, put down any combination of Indians that might be formed against them.   In other words, it was then made evident that English colonists would certainly be safe in the new world, and also that they would not always be colonists."

While the end of an historical or literary era cannot always be thus conveniently indicated by a date, there is no doubt that the final quarter of the seventeenth century witnessed deep changes in the outward life and the inner temper of the colonists. The "first fine careless rapture" was over.   Only a few aged men could recall the memory of the first settlements.   Between the founding of Jamestown and the rebellion under the leadership of Nathaniel Bacon almost seventy years had intervened, an interval corresponding to that which separates us from the Mexican War.   Roger Wil-

liams ended his much-enduring and beneficent
life in the flourishing town of Providence in 1684.
He had already outlived Cotton and Hooker,
Shepard and Winthrop, by more than thirty years.
Inevitably men began, toward the end of the century, to take stock of the great venture of coloniza-
tion, to scrutinize their own history and present
position, to ask searching questions of themselves.
"You have better food and raiment than was in
former times," wrote the aged Roger Clark, in 1676;
"but have you better hearts than your forefathers
had?" Thomas Walley's *Languishing Commonwealth* maintains that "Faith is dead, and Love is
cold, and Zeal is gone." Urian Oakes's election
sermon of 1670 in Cambridge is a condemnation of
the prevalent worldliness and ostentation. This
period of critical inquiry and assessment, however,
also gives grounds for just pride. History, biography, eulogy, are flourishing. The reader is
reminded of that epoch, one hundred and fifty
years later, when the deaths of John Adams and
of Thomas Jefferson, falling upon the same anni-
versary day, the Fourth of July, 1826, stirred all
Americans to a fresh recognition of the services
wrought by the Fathers of the Republic. So it was
in the colonies at the close of the seventeenth cen-

tury. Old England, in one final paroxysm of political disgust, cast out the last Stuart in 1688. That Revolution marks, as we have seen, the close of a long and tragic struggle which began in the autocratic theories of James the First and in the absolutism of Charles. Almost every phase of that momentous conflict had its reverberation across the Atlantic, as the history of the granting and withdrawal of colonial charters witnesses abundantly. The American pioneers were quite aware of what was going on in England, and they praised God or grumbled, thriftily profited by the results or quietly nullified them, as the case might be. But all the time, while England was rocked to its foundations, the colonists struck steadily forward into their own independent life.

CHAPTER III

WHEN the eighteenth century opened, many signs of change were in the air. The third generation of native-born Americans was becoming secularized. The theocracy of New England had failed. In the height of the tragic folly over the supposed "witchcraft" in Salem, Increase Mather and his son Cotton had held up the hands of the judges in their implacable work. But before five years had passed, Judge Sewall does public penance in church for his share of the awful blunder, desiring "to take the shame and blame of it." Robert Calef's cool pamphlet exposing the weakness of the prosecutors' case is indeed burned by Increase Mather in the Harvard Yard, but the liberal party are soon to force Mather from the Presidency and to refuse that office to his son. In the town of Boston, once hermetically sealed against heresy, there are Baptist and Episcopal churches — and a dancing-master.   Young Benjamin Franklin, born in 1706, professes a high respect for the Mathers, but he does not go to church, "Sunday being my studying day," and neither the clerical nor the secular arm of Boston is long enough and strong enough to compel that industrious apprentice into piety.

If such was the state of New England, the laxity of New York and Virginia needs little evidence. Contemporary travelers found the New Yorkers singularly attached to the things of this present world.   Philadelphia was prosperous and therewith content.   Virginia was a paradise with no forbidden fruit.   Hugh Jones, writing of it in 1724, considers North Carolina "the refuge of runaways," and South Carolina "the delight of buccaneers and pirates," but Virginia "the happy retreat of true Britons and true Churchmen." Unluckily these Virginians, well nourished "by the plenty of the country," have "contemptible notions of England!"   We shall hear from them again.   In the meantime the witty William Byrd of Westover describes for us his amusing survey of the Dismal Swamp, and his excursions into North Carolina and to Governor Spotswood's iron mines, where he reads aloud to the Widow Fleming, on a rainy autumn day, three acts of the *Beggars'*

Opera, just over from London. So runs the world away, south of the Potomac. Thackeray paints it once for all, no doubt, in the opening chapters of *The Virginians.*

To discover any ambitious literary effort in this period, we must turn northward again. In the middle colonies, and especially in Philadelphia, which had now outgrown Boston in population, there was a quickened interest in education and science. But the New Englanders were still the chief makers of books. Three great names will sufficiently represent the age: Cotton Mather, a prodigy of learning whose eyes turn back fondly to the provincial past; Jonathan Edwards, perhaps the most consummate intellect of the eighteenth century; and Benjamin Franklin, certainly the most perfect exponent of its many-sided life.

When Cotton Mather was graduated from Harvard in 1678, in his sixteenth year, he was publicly complimented by President Oakes, in fulsome Latin, as the grandson of Richard Mather and John Cotton. This atmosphere of flattery, this consciousness of continuing in his own person the famous local dynasty, surrounded and sustained him to the end. He had a less commanding personality than his father Increase. His nervous sensibility was excessive. His natural vanity was never subdued, though it was often chastened by trial and bitter disappointment. But, like his father, he was an omnivorous reader and a facile producer of books, carrying daily such burdens of mental and spiritual excitement as would have crushed a normal man. Increase Mather published some one hundred and fifty books and pamphlets: Cotton Mather not less than four hundred. The Rev. John Norton, in his sketch of John Cotton, remarks that "the hen, which brings not forth without uncessant sitting night and day, is an apt emblem of students." Certainly the hen is an apt emblem of the "uncessant" sitter, the credulous scratcher, the fussy cackler who produced the *Magnalia*.

Yet he had certain elements of greatness. His tribal loyalty was perfect. His ascetic devotion to his conception of religious truth was absolute. His *Diary*, which has recently been published in full, records his concern for the chief political events in Europe in his day, no less than his brooding solicitude for the welfare of his townspeople, and his agony of spirit over the lapses of his wayward eldest son. A "sincere" man, then, as Carlyle would say, at bottom; but overlaid with such

"Jewish old clothes," such professional robings and personal plumage as makes it difficult, save in the revealing *Diary*, to see the man himself.

The *Magnalia Christi Americana*, treating the history of New England from 1620 to 1698, was published in a tall London folio of nearly 800 pages in 1702. It is divided into seven books, and proceeds, by methods entirely unique, to tell of Pilgrim and Puritan divines and governors, of Harvard College, of the churches of New England, of marvelous events, of Indian wars; and in general to justify, as only a member of the Mather dynasty could justify, the ways of God to Boston men. Hawthorne and Whittier, Longfellow and Lowell knew this book well and found much honey in the vast carcass. To have had four such readers and a biographer like Barrett Wendell must be gratifying to Cotton Mather in Paradise.

The *Diary* of Mather's fellow-townsman Judge Samuel Sewall has been read more generally in recent years than anything written by Mather himself. It was begun in 1673, nine years earlier than the first entry in Mather's *Diary*, and it ends in 1729, while Mather's closes in 1724. As a picture of everyday happenings in New England, Sewall's *Diary* is as far superior to Mather's as

Pepys's *Diary* is to George Fox's *Journal* in painting the England of the Restoration. Samuel Sewall was an admirably solid figure, keen, forceful, honest. Most readers of his *Diary* believe that he really was in luck when he was rejected by the Widow Winthrop on that fateful November day when his eye noted — in spite of his infatuation — that "her dress was not so clean as sometime it had been. Jehovah Jireh!"

One pictures Cotton Mather as looking instinctively backward to the Heroic Age of New England with pious nervous exaltation, and Samuel Sewall as doing the day's work uprightly without taking anxious thought of either past or future. But Jonathan Edwards is set apart from these and other men. He is a lonely seeker after spiritual perfection, in quest of that city "far on the world's rim," as Masefield says of it, the city whose builder and maker is God.

The story of Edwards's career has the simplicity and dignity of tragedy. Born in a parsonage in the quiet Connecticut valley in 1703 — the year of John Wesley's birth—he is writing at the age of ten to disprove the doctrine of the materiality of the soul. At twelve he is studying "the wondrous way of the working of the spider," with a precision and enthusiasm which would have made him a great naturalist. At fourteen he begins his notes on *The Mind* and on *Natural Science*. He is graduated from Yale in 1720, studies theology, and at twenty-four becomes the colleague of his famous grandfather, Solomon Stoddard, in the church at Northampton. He marries the beautiful Sarah Pierrepont, whom he describes in his journal in a prose rhapsody which, like his mystical rhapsodies on religion in the same youthful period, glows with a clear unearthly beauty unmatched in any English prose of that century. For twenty-three years he serves the Northampton church, and his sermons win him the rank of the foremost preacher in New England. John Wesley reads at Oxford his account of the great revival of 1735. Whitefield comes to visit him at Northampton. Then, in 1750, the ascetic preacher alienates his church over issues pertaining to discipline and to the administration of the sacrament. He is dismissed. He preaches his "farewell sermon," like Wesley, like Emerson, like Newman, and many another still unborn. He removes to Stockbridge, then a hamlet in the wilderness, preaches to the Indians, and writes treatises on theology and metaphysics, among them the world-

4

famous *Freedom of the Will*. In 1757, upon the death of his son-in-law, President Aaron Burr of Princeton, Edwards is called to the vacant Presidency. He is reluctant to go, for though he is only fifty-four, his health has never been robust, and he has his great book on the *History of Redemption* still to write. But he accepts, finds the smallpox raging in Princeton upon his arrival in January, 1758, is inoculated, and dies of the disease in March — his dreams unfulfilled, his life-work once more thwarted. Close by the tomb of this saint is the tomb of his grandson, Aaron Burr, who killed Hamilton.

The literary reputation of Jonathan Edwards has turned, like the vicissitudes of his life, upon factors that could not be foreseen. His contemporary fame was chiefly as a preacher, and was due to sermons like those upon *God Glorified in Man's Dependence* and *The Reality of Spiritual Life*, rather than to such discourses as the Enfield sermon, *Sinners in the Hands of an Angry God*, which in our own day is the best known of his deliverances. Legends have grown up around this terrific Enfield sermon. Its fearful power over its immediate hearers cannot be gainsaid, and it will long continue to be quoted as an example of the length to which a Calvinistic logician of genius was compelled by his own scheme to go. We still see the tall, sweet-faced man, worn by his daily twelve hours of intense mental toil, leaning on one elbow in the pulpit and reading from manuscript, without even raising his gentle voice, those words which smote his congregation into spasms of terror and which seem to us sheer blasphemy.

Yet the *Farewell Sermon* of 1750 gives a more characteristic view of Edwards's mind and heart, and conveys an ineffaceable impression of his nobility of soul. His diction, like Wordsworth's, is usually plain almost to bareness; the formal framework of his discourses is obtruded; and he hunts objections to their last hiding-place with wearisome pertinacity. Yet his logic is incandescent. Steel sometimes burns to the touch like this, in the bitter winters of New England, and one wonders whether Edwards's brain was not of ice, so pitiless does it seem. His treatise denying the freedom of the will has given him a European reputation comparable with that enjoyed by Franklin in science and Jefferson in political propaganda. It was really a polemic demonstrating the sovereignty of God, rather than pure theology or metaphysics. Edwards goes beyond

Augustine and Calvin in asserting the arbitrary will of the Most High and in "denying to the human will any self-determining power." He has been refuted by events and tendencies, such as the growth of historical criticism and the widespread acceptance of the doctrine of evolution, rather than by the might of any single antagonist. So, too, the Dred Scott decision of Chief Justice Taney, holding that the slave was not a citizen, was not so much answered by opponents as it was superseded by the arbitrament of war. But the idealism of this lonely thinker has entered deeply and permanently into the spiritual life of his countrymen, and he will continue to be read by a few of those who still read Plato and Dante.

"My mother grieves," wrote Benjamin Franklin to his father in 1738, "that one of her sons is an Arian, another an Arminian. What an Arminian or an Arian is, I cannot say that I very well know. The truth is I make such distinctions very little my study." To understand Franklin's indifference to such distinctions, we must realize how completely he represents the secularizing tendencies of his age. What a drama of worldly adventure it all was, this roving life of the tallow-chandler's son, who runs away from home, walks the streets of Philadelphia with the famous loaves of bread under his arm, is diligent in business, slips over to London, where he gives lessons in swimming and in total abstinence, slips back to Philadelphia and becomes its leading citizen, fights the long battle of the American colonies in London, sits in the Continental Congress, sails to Europe to arrange that French Alliance which brought our Revolution to a successful issue, and comes home at last, full of years and honors, to a bland and philosophical exit from the stage!

He broke with every Puritan tradition. The Franklins were relatively late comers to New England. They sprang from a long line of blacksmiths at Ecton in Northamptonshire. The seat of the Washingtons was not far away, and Franklin's latest biographer points out that the pink-coated huntsmen of the Washington gentry may often have stopped at Ecton to have their horses shod at the Franklin smithy. Benjamin's father came out in 1685, more than fifty years after the most notable Puritan emigration. Young Benjamin, born in 1706, was as untouched by the ardors of that elder generation as he would have been by the visions of Dante — an author, by the way, whom he never mentions, even as he never mentions Shakespeare. He had no reverence for Puritan New England. To its moral beauty, its fine severity, he was wholly blind. As a boy he thriftily sold his *Pilgrim's Progress*. He became, in the new fashion of that day, a Deist. Like a true child of the eighteenth century, his attitude toward the seventeenth was that of amused or contemptuous superiority. Thackeray has somewhere a charming phrase about his own love for the back seat of the stage-coach, the seat which, in the old coaching days, gave one a view of the receding landscape. Thackeray, like Burke before him, loved historical associations, historical sentiment, the backward look over the long road which humanity has traveled. But Franklin faced the other way. He would have endorsed his friend Jefferson's scornful sentence, "The dead have no rights." He joined himself wholly to that eighteenth century in which his own lot was cast, and, alike in his qualities and in his defects, he became one of its most perfect representatives.

To catch the full spirit of that age, turn for an instant to the London of 1724 — the year of Franklin's arrival. Thirty-six years have elapsed since the glorious Revolution of 1688; the Whig principles, then triumphant, have been tacitly accepted by both political parties; the Jacobite revolt of 1715 has proved a fiasco; the country has accepted the House of Hanover and a government by party leadership of the House of Commons, and it does not care whether Sir Robert Walpole buys a few rotten boroughs, so long as he maintains peace with Europe and prosperity at home. England is weary of seventeenth century "enthusiasm," weary of conflict, sick of idealism. She has found in the accepted Whig principles a satisfactory compromise, a working theory of society, a *modus vivendi* which nobody supposes is perfect but which will answer the prayer appointed to be read in all the churches, "Grant us peace in our time, O Lord." The theories to which men gave their lives in the seventeenth century seem ghostly in their unreality; but the prize turnips on Sir Robert's Norfolk farm, and the wines in his cellar, and the offices at his disposal — these are very real indeed. London merchants are making money; the squire and the parson are tranquilly ruling the country parishes; the philosophy of John Locke is everywhere triumphant. Mr. Pope is the poet of the hour, and his *Essay on Man*, counseling acceptance of our mortal situation, is considered to be the last word of human wisdom and of poetical elegance. In prose, the style of the *Spectator* rules — an admirable style, Franklin thought, and he imitated it patiently until its ease and urbanity had become his own. And indeed, how much of that London of the third decade of the century passed into the mind of the inquisitive, roving, loose-living printer's apprentice from Philadelphia! It taught him that the tangible world is the real world, and that nothing succeeds like success; but it never even whispered to him that sometimes nothing damns like success.

In his limitations, no less than in his power of assimilation, Franklin was the representative man of his era. He had no artistic interests, no liking for metaphysics after his brief devotion, in early manhood, to the dialogues of Plato. He taught himself some Latin, but he came to believe that the classics had little significance and that they should be superseded by the modern languages. For the mediæval world he had no patience or understanding. To these defects of his century we must add some failings of his own. He was not always truthful. He had an indelible streak of coarseness. His conception of the "art of virtue" was mechanical. When Carlyle called Franklin the "father of all the Yankees," we must remember that the Scotch prophet hated Yankees and believed that Franklin's smooth, plausible, trader type of morality was only a broad way to the everlasting bonfire.

But it is folly to linger over the limitations of the tallow-chandler's son. The catalogue of his beneficent activity is a vast one. Balzac once characterized him as the man who invented the lightning-rod, the hoax, and the republic. His contributions to science have to do with electricity, earthquakes, geology, meteorology, physics, chemistry, astronomy, mathematics, navigation of air and water, agriculture, medicine, and hygiene. In some of these fields he did pioneer work of lasting significance. His teachings of thrift and prudence, as formulated in the maxims of Poor Richard, gave him a world-wide reputation. He attacked war, like Voltaire, not so much for its wickedness as for its folly, and cheerfully gave up many years of a long life to the effort to promote a better understanding among the nations of the world.

It is perhaps needless to add what all persons who love good writing know, that Benjamin Franklin was a most delightful writer. His letters cover an amusing and extraordinary variety of topics. He ranges from balloons to summer hats, and from the advantages of deep ploughing to bifocal glasses, which, by the way, he invented. He argues for sharp razors and cold baths, and for fresh air in the sleeping-room. He discusses the morals of the game of chess, the art of swimming, the evils of smoky chimneys, the need of reformed spelling. Indeed, his passion for improvement led him not only to try his hand upon an abridgment of the Book of Common Prayer, but to go even so far as to propose seriously a new rendering of the Lord's Prayer. His famous proposal for a new version of the Bible, however, which Matthew Arnold solemnly held up to reprobation, was only a joke which Matthew Arnold did not see — the new version of Job being, in fact, a clever bit of political satire against party leadership in England. Even more brilliant examples of his skill in political satire are his imaginary *Edict of the King of Prussia against England*, and his famous *Rules for Reducing a Great Empire to a Small One*. But I must not try to call the roll of all the good things in Franklin's ten volumes. I will simply say that those who know Franklin only in his *Autobiography*, charming as that classic production is, have made but an imperfect acquaintance with the range, the vitality, the vigor of this admirable craftsman who chose a style "smooth, clear, and short," and made it serve every purpose of his versatile and beneficent mind.

When the passage of the Stamp Act in 1765 startled the American colonies out of their provincial sense of security and made them aware of their real attitude toward the mother country, Franklin was in London. Eleven years earlier, in 1754, he had offered a plan for the *Union of the Colonies*, but this had not contemplated separation from England. It was rather what we should call a scheme for imperial federation under the British Crown. We may use his word union, however, in a different field from that of politics. How much union of sentiment, of mental and moral life, of literary, educational, and scientific endeavor, was there in the colonies when the hour of self-examination came? Only the briefest summary may be attempted here.

As to race, these men of the third and fourth generation since the planting of the colonies were by no means so purely English as the first settlers. The 1,600,000 colonists in 1760 were mingled of many stocks, the largest non-English elements being German and Scotch-Irish — that is, Scotch who had settled for a while in Ulster before emigrating to America. "About one-third of the colonists in 1760," says Professor Channing, "were born outside of America." Crèvecœur's *Letters from an American Farmer* thus defined the Americans: "They are a mixture of English, Scotch, Irish, French, Dutch, Germans, and Swedes. From this promiscuous breed that race now called Americans has arisen." The Atlantic seaboard, with a narrow strip inland, was fairly well covered by local communities, differing in blood, in religion, in political organization— "a congeries of separate experiments" or young utopias, waiting for that most utopian experiment of all, a federal union. But the dominant language of the "promiscuous breed" was English, and in the few real centers of intellectual life the English tradition was almost absolute.

The merest glance at colonial journalism will confirm this estimate. The *Boston News-Letter*, begun in 1704, was the first of the journals, if we omit the single issue of *Publick Occurrences* in the same town in 1690. By 1765 there were nearly fifty colonial newspapers and several magazines. Their influence made for union, in Franklin's sense of that word, and their literary models, like their paper, type, and even ink, were found in London. The *New England Courant*, established in Boston in 1721 by James Franklin, is full of imitations of the *Tatler*, *Spectator*, and *Guardian*. What is more, the *Courant* boasted of its office collection of books, including Shakespeare, Milton, the *Spectator*, and Swift's *Tale of a Tub*.[1] This was in 1722. If we remember that no allusion to Shakespeare has been discovered in the colonial literature of the seventeenth century, and scarcely an allusion to the Puritan poet Milton, and that the Harvard College Library in 1723 had nothing of Addison, Steele, Bolingbroke, Dryden, Pope, and Swift, and had only recently obtained copies of Milton and Shakespeare, we can appreciate the value of James Franklin's apprenticeship in London. Perhaps we can even forgive him for that attack upon the Mathers which threw the conduct of the *Courant*, for a brief period, into the hands of his brother Benjamin, whose turn at a London apprenticeship was soon to come.

If we follow this younger brother to Philadelphia and to Bradford's *American Mercury* or

[1] Cook, E. C. *Literary Influences in Colonial Newspapers, 1704-1750.* N. Y., 1912.

to Franklin's own *Pennsylvania Gazette*, or if we study the *Gazettes* of Maryland, Virginia, and South Carolina, the impression is still the same. The literary news is still chiefly from London, from two months to a year late. London books are imported and reprinted. Franklin reprints *Pamela*, and his Library Company of Philadelphia has two copies of *Paradise Lost* for circulation in 1741, whereas there had been no copy of that work in the great library of Cotton Mather. American journalism then, as now, owed its vitality to a secular spirit of curiosity about the actual world. It followed England as its model, but it was beginning to develop a temper of its own.

Colonial education and colonial science were likewise chiefly indebted to London, but by 1751 Franklin's papers on electricity began to repay the loan. A university club in New York in 1745 could have had but fifteen members at most, for these were all the "academics" in town. Yet Harvard had then been sending forth her graduates for more than a century. William and Mary was founded in 1693, Yale in 1701, Princeton in 1746, King's (now Columbia) in 1754, the University of Pennsylvania in 1755, and Brown in 1764. These colonial colleges were mainly in the hands of clergymen. They tended to reproduce a type of scholarship based upon the ancient languages. The curriculum varied but little in the different colonies, and this fact helped to produce a feeling of fellowship among all members of the republic of letters. The men who debated the Stamp Act were, with a few striking exceptions, men trained in Latin and Greek, familiar with the great outlines of human history, accustomed to the discipline of academic disputation. They knew the ideas and the vocabulary of cultivated Europe and were conscious of no provincial inferiority. In the study of the physical sciences, likewise, the colonials were but little behind the mother country. The Royal Society had its distinguished members here. The Mathers, the Dudleys, John Winthrop of Connecticut, John Bartram, James Logan, James Godfrey, Cadwallader Colden, and above all, Franklin himself, were winning the respect of European students, and were teaching Americans to use their eyes and their minds not merely upon the records of the past but in searching out the inexhaustible meanings of the present. There is no more fascinating story than that of the beginnings of American science in and outside of the colleges, and this movement, like the influence of journalism and of the higher education, counted for colonial union.

Professor Tyler, our foremost literary student of the period, summarizes the characteristics of colonial literature in these words: "Before the year 1765, we find in this country, not one American people, but many American peoples. . . . No cohesive principle prevailed, no centralizing life; each little nation was working out its own destiny in its own fashion." But he adds that with that year the colonial isolation came to an end, and that the student must thereafter "deal with the literature of one multitudinous people, variegated, indeed, in personal traits, but single in its commanding ideas and in its national destinies." It is easy to be wise after the event. Yet there was living in London in 1765, as the agent for Pennsylvania, a shrewd and bland Colonial — an honorary M.A. from both Harvard and Yale, a D.C.L. of Oxford and an LL.D. of St. Andrews — who was by no means sure that the Stamp Act meant the end of Colonialism. And Franklin's uncertainty was shared by Washington. When the tall Virginian took command of the Continental Army as late as 1775, he "abhorred the idea of independence." Nevertheless John Jay, writing the second number of the *Federalist* in 1787, only twelve years later, could say: "Providence has been pleased to give this one connected country to one united people; a people descended from the same ancestors, speaking the same language, professing the same religion, attached to the same principles of government."

5

CHAPTER IV

THE REVOLUTION

IF we turn, however, to the literature produced in America between the passage of the Stamp Act in 1765 and the adoption of the Constitution in 1787, we perceive that it is a literature of discord and passion. Its spirit is not that of "one united people." Washington could indeed declare in his *Farewell Address* of 1796, "With slight shades of difference, you have the same religion, manners, habits, and political principles"; yet no one knew better than Washington upon what a slender thread this political unity had often hung, and how impossible it had been to foresee the end from the beginning.

It is idle to look in the writings of the Revolutionary period for the literature of beauty, for a quiet harmonious unfolding of the deeper secrets of life. It was a time of swift and pitiless change, of action rather than reflection, of the turning

66

of many separate currents into one headlong stream. "We must, indeed, all hang together," runs Franklin's well-known witticism in Independence Hall, "or, most assuredly, we shall all hang separately." Excellently spoken, Doctor! And that homely, cheery, daring sentence gives the keynote of much of the Revolutionary writing that has survived. It may be heard in the state papers of Samuel Adams, the oratory of Patrick Henry, the pamphlets of Thomas Paine, the satires of Freneau and Trumbull, and in the subtle, insinuating, thrilling paragraphs of Thomas Jefferson.

We can only glance in passing at the literature of the Lost Cause, the Loyalist or "Tory" pleadings for allegiance to Britain. It was written by able and honest men, like Boucher and Odell, Seabury, Leonard and Galloway. They distrusted what Seabury called "our sovereign Lord the Mob." They represented, in John Adams's opinion, nearly one-third of the people of the colonies, and recent students believe that this estimate was too low. In some colonies the Loyalists were clearly in the majority. In all they were a menacing element, made up of the conservative, the prosperous, the well-educated, with a mixture, of course, of mere placemen and tuft-hunters. They composed weighty pamphlets, eloquent sermons, and sparkling satire in praise of the old order of things. When their cause was lost forever, they wrote gossipy letters from their exile in London or pathetic verses in their new home in Nova Scotia and Ontario. Their place in our national life and literature has never been filled, and their talents and virtues are never likely to receive adequate recognition. They took the wrong fork of the road.

There were gentle spirits, too, in this period, endowed with delicate literary gifts, but quite unsuited for the clash of controversy — members, in Crèvecœur's touching words, of the "secret communion among good men throughout the world." "I am a lover of peace, what must I do?" asks Crèvecœur in his *Letters from an American Farmer*. "I was happy before this unfortunate Revolution. I feel that I am no longer so, therefore I regret the change. My heart sometimes seems tired with beating, it wants rest like my eyelids, which feel oppressed with so many watchings." Crèvecœur, an immigrant from Normandy, was certainly no weakling, but he felt that the great idyllic American adventure — which he described so captivatingly in his chapter entitled *What is an American* — was ending tragically in civil war. Another white-souled itinerant of that day was John Woolman of New Jersey, whose *Journal*, praised by Charles Lamb and Channing and edited by Whittier, is finding more readers in the twentieth century than it won in the nineteenth. "A man unlettered," said Whittier, "but with natural refinement and delicate sense of fitness, the purity of whose heart enters into his language." Woolman died at fifty-two in far-away York, England, whither he had gone to attend a meeting of the Society of Friends.

The three tall volumes of the Princeton edition of the poems of Philip Freneau bear the sub-title, "Poet of the American Revolution." But our Revolution, in truth, never had an adequate poet. The prose-men, such as Jefferson, rose nearer the height of the great argument than did the men of rhyme. Here and there the struggle inspired a brisk ballad like Francis Hopkinson's *Battle of the Kegs*, a Hudibrastic satire like Trumbull's *McFingal*, or a patriotic song like Timothy Dwight's *Columbia*. Freneau painted from his own experience the horrors of the British prison-ship, and celebrated, in cadences learned from Gray and Collins, the valor of the men who fell at Eutaw

Springs.   There was patriotic verse in extraordinary profusion, but its literary value is slight, and
it reveals few moods of the American mind that
are not more perfectly conveyed through oratory,
the pamphlet, and the political essay.   The immediate models of this Revolutionary verse were
the minor British bards of the eighteenth century, a century greatly given to verse-writing,
but endowed by Heaven with the "prose-reason"
mainly.   The reader of Burton E. Stevenson's
collection of *Poems of American History* can easily
compare the contemporary verse inspired by the
events of the Revolution with the modern verse
upon the same historic themes.   He will see how
slenderly equipped for song were most of the later
eighteenth-century Americans and how unfavorable to poetry was the tone of that hour.

Freneau himself suffered, throughout his long
career, from the depressing indifference of his
public to the true spirit of poetry.   "An old
college mate of mine," said James Madison — who
was by tradition Freneau's room-mate at Princeton in the class of 1771 — "a poet and man of
literary and refined tastes, knowing nothing of the
world."   When but three years out of college,
the cautious Madison wrote to another friend:

"Poetry wit and Criticism Romances Plays &c
captivated me much: but I begin to discover
that they deserve but a moderate portion of
a mortal's Time and that something more substantial more durable more profitable befits
our riper age." Madison was then at the ripe
age of twenty-three! Professor Pattee, Freneau's editor, quotes these words to illustrate the
"common sense" atmosphere of the age which
proved fatal to Freneau's development. Yet
the sturdy young New Yorker, of Huguenot de-
scent, is a charming figure, and his later malevo-
lence was shown only to his political foes. After
leaving Princeton he tries teaching, the law, the
newspaper, the sea; he is aflame with patriotic
zeal; he writes, like most American poets, far
too much for his own reputation. As the editor of
the *National Gazette* in Philadelphia, he becomes
involved in the bitter quarrel between his chief,
Jefferson, and Alexander Hamilton. His attachment to the cause of the French Revolution makes
him publish baseless attacks upon Washington.
By and by he retires to a New Jersey farm, still
toying with journalism, still composing verses.
He turns patriotic poet once more in the War of
1812; but the public has now forgotten him.

He lives on in poverty and seclusion, and in his eightieth year loses his way in a snowstorm and perishes miserably — this in 1832, the year of the death of the great Sir Walter Scott, who once had complimented Freneau by borrowing one of his best lines of poetry.

It is in the orations and pamphlets and state-papers inspired by the Revolutionary agitation that we find the most satisfactory expression of the thought and feeling of that generation. Its typical literature is civic rather than æsthetic, a sort of writing which has been incidental to the accomplishing of some political, social, or moral purpose, and which scarcely regards itself as literature at all. James Otis's argument against the Writs of Assistance in Massachusetts in 1761, and Patrick Henry's speech in the Virginia House of Burgesses in 1765, mark epochs in the emotional life of these communities. They were reported imperfectly or not at all, but they can no more be ignored in an assessment of our national experience than editorials, sermons, or conversations which have expressed the deepest feelings of a day and then have perished beyond resurrection.

Yet if natural orators like Otis and Henry be denied a strictly "literary" rating because their surviving words are obviously inadequate to account for the popular effect of their speeches, it is still possible to measure the efficiency of the pamphleteer. When John Adams tells us that "James Otis was Isaiah and Ezekiel united," we must take his word for the impression which Otis's oratory left upon his mind. But John Adams's own writings fill ten stout volumes which invite our judgment. The "truculent and sarcastic splendor" of his hyperboles need not blind us to his real literary excellencies, such as clearness, candor, vigor of phrase, freshness of idea. A testy, rugged, "difficult" person was John Adams, but he grew mellower with age, and his latest letters and journals are full of whimsical charm.

John Adams's cousin Samuel was not precisely a charming person. Bigoted, tireless, secretive, this cunning manipulator of political passions followed many tortuous paths. His ability for adroit misstatement of an adversary's position has been equaled but once in our history. But to the casual reader of his four volumes, Samuel Adams seems ever to be breathing the liberal air of the town-meeting: everything is as plainly obvious as a good citizen can make it. He has, too, the large utterance of the European liberalism of his day.

"Resolved," read his Resolutions of the House of Representatives of Massachusetts in 1765, "that there are certain essential rights of the British constitution of government which are founded in the law of God and nature and are the common rights of mankind." In his statement of the Rights of the Colonists (1772) we are assured that "among the natural rights of the colonists are these, First, a right to Life; secondly to Liberty; thirdly to Property. . . . All men have a Right to remain in a State of Nature as long as they please. . . . When Men enter into Society, it is by voluntary consent." Jean-Jacques himself could not be more bland, nor at heart more fiercely demagogic.

"Tom" Paine would have been no match for "Sam" Adams in a town-meeting, but he was an even greater pamphleteer. He had arrived from England in 1774, at the age of thirty-eight, having hitherto failed in most of his endeavors for a livelihood. "Rebellious Staymaker; unkempt," says Carlyle; but General Charles Lee noted that there was "genius in his eyes," and he bore a letter of introduction from Franklin commending him as an "ingenious, worthy young man," which obtained for him a position on the *Pennsylvania Magazine*. Before he had been a year on American soil, Paine was writing the most famous pamphlet of our political literature, *Common Sense*, which appeared in January, 1776. "A style hitherto unknown on this side of the Atlantic," wrote Edmund Randolph. Yet this style of familiar talk to the crowd had been used seventy years earlier by Defoe and Swift, and it was to be employed again by a gaunt American frontiersman who was born in 1809, the year of Thomas Paine's death. *The Crisis*, a series of thirteen pamphlets, of which the first was issued in December, 1776, seemed to justify the contemporary opinion that the "American cause owed as much to the pen of Paine as to the sword of Washington." Paine, who was now serving in the army, might have heard his own words, "These are the times that try men's souls," read aloud, by Washington's orders, to the ragged troops just before they crossed the Delaware to win the victory of Trenton. The best known productions of Paine's subsequent career, *The Rights of Man* and *The Age of Reason*, were written in Europe, but they were read throughout America. The reputation of the "rebellious Staymaker" has suffered from certain grimy habits and from the ridiculous charge of atheism. He was no more an atheist than Franklin or Jefferson. In no sense an original thinker, he could impart to outworn shreds of deistic controversy and to shallow generalizations about democracy a personal fervor which transformed them and made his pages gay and bold and clear as a trumpet.

Clear and bold and gay was Alexander Hamilton likewise; and his literary services to the Revolution are less likely to be underestimated than Thomas Paine's. They began with that boyish speech in "the Fields" of New York City in 1774 and with *The Farmer Refuted*, a reply to Samuel Seabury's *Westchester Farmer*. They were continued in extraordinary letters, written during Hamilton's military career, upon the defects of the Articles of Confederation and of the finances of the Confederation. Hamilton contributed but little to the actual structure of the new Constitution, but as a debater he fought magnificently and triumphantly for its adoption by the Convention of the State of New York in 1788. Together with Jay and Madison he defended the fundamental principles of the Federal Union in the remarkable series of papers known as the *Federalist*. These eighty-five papers, appearing over the signature "Publius" in two New York newspapers between October, 1787, and April, 1788, owed their conception largely to Hamilton, who wrote more than half of them himself. In manner they are not unlike the substantial Whig literature of England, and in political theory they have little in common with the Revolutionary literature which we have been considering. The reasoning is close, the style vigorous but neither warmed by passion nor colored by the individual emotions of the author. The *Federalist* remains a classic example of the civic quality of our post-Revolutionary American political writing, broadly social in its outlook, well informed as to the past, confident — but not reckless — of the future. Many Americans still read it who would be shocked by Tom Paine and bored with Edmund Burke. It has none of the literary genius of either of those writers, but its formative influence upon successive generations of political thinking has been steadying and sound.

In fact, our citizen literature cannot be understood aright if one fails to observe that its effect has often turned, not upon mere verbal skill, but upon the weight of character behind the words. Thus the grave and reserved George Washington says of the Constitution of 1787: "Let us raise a standard to which the wise and the honest can repair; the event is in the hand of God." The whole personality of the great Virginian is back of that simple, perfect sentence. It brings us to our feet, like a national anthem.

One American, no doubt our most gifted man of letters of that century, passed most of the Revolutionary period abroad, in the service of his country. Benjamin Franklin was fifty-nine in the year of the Stamp Act. When he returned from France in 1785 he was seventy-nine, but he was still writing as admirably as ever when he died at eighty-four. We cannot dismiss this singular, varied, and fascinating American better than by quoting the letter which George Washington wrote to him in September, 1789. It has the dignity and formality of the eighteenth century, but it is warm with tested friendship and it glows with deep human feeling: "If to be venerated for benevolence, if to be admired for talents, if to be esteemed for patriotism, if to be beloved for philanthropy, can gratify the human mind, you must have the pleasing consolation to know that you have not lived in vain. And I flatter myself that it will not be ranked among the least grateful occurrences of your life to be assured, that, so long as I retain my memory, you will be recollected with respect, veneration, and affection by your sincere friend, George Washington."

There remains another Virginian, the symbol of the Revolutionary age, the author of words more widely known around the globe than any other words penned by an American. "Thomas Jefferson," writes the latest of his successors in the Presidency, "was not a man of the people, but he was a man of such singular insight that he saw that all the roots of generous power come from the people." On his father's side Jefferson came from sound yeoman stock, in which Welsh blood ran. His mother was a Virginia Randolph. Born in Albemarle County, near the "little mountain" — Monticello — where he built a mansion for his bride and where he lies buried, the tall, strong, red-haired, gray-eyed, gifted boy was reputed the best shot, the best rider, the best fiddle-player in the county. He studied hard at William and Mary over his Greek, Latin, French, Italian, and Spanish, but he also frequented the best society of the little capital. He learned to call himself a Deist and to theorize about ideal commonwealths. There was already in him that latent radicalism which made him strike down, as soon as he had the power, two of the fundamental principles of the society into which he was born, the principle of entailed property and that of church establishment.

Such was the youth of twenty-two who was thrilled in 1765 by the Stamp Act. In the ten years of passionate discussion which followed, two things became clear: first, that there had long existed among the colonists very radical theoretical notions of political freedom; and second, that there was everywhere a spirit of practical conservatism. Jefferson illustrates the union of these two tendencies.

He took his seat in the Continental Congress in June, 1775. He was only thirty-two, but he had already written, in the summer of 1774, *A Summary View of the Rights of British America* which had been published in England by Burke, himself a judge of good writing and sound politics. Jefferson had also prepared in 1775 the *Address of the Virginia House of Burgesses.* For these reasons he was placed at the head of the Committee for drafting the Declaration of Independence. We need not linger over the familiar circumstances of its composition. Everybody knows how Franklin and Adams made a few verbal alterations in the first draft, how the committee of five then reported it to the Congress, which proceeded to cut out about one-fourth of the matter, while Franklin tried to comfort the writhing author with his cheerful story about the sign of John Thompson the hatter. Forty-seven years afterwards, in reply to the charge of lack of originality brought against the Declaration by Timothy Pickering and John Adams — charges which have been repeated at intervals ever since — Jefferson replied philosophically: "Whether I gathered my ideas from reading or reflection I do not know. I know only that I turned neither to book nor pamphlet while writing it. I did not consider it as any part of my charge to invent new ideas altogether and to offer no sentiment which had ever been expressed before." O wise young man, and fundamentally Anglo-Saxon young man, to turn his back, in that crisis, to the devil of mere cleverness, and stick to recognized facts and accepted sentiments! But his pen retains its cunning in spite of him; and the drop of hot Welsh blood tells; and the cosmopolitan reading and thinking tell; and they transform what Pickering called a "commonplace compilation, its sentiments hackneyed in Congress for two years before," into an immortal manifesto to mankind.

Its method is the simplest. The preamble is

6

philosophical, dealing with "self-evident" truths. Today the men who dislike or doubt these truths dismiss the preamble as "theoretical," or, to use another term of derogation favored by reactionaries, "French." But if the preamble be French and philosophical, the specific charges against the King are very English and practical. Here are certain facts, presented no doubt with consummate rhetorical skill, but facts, undeniably. The Anglo-Saxon in Jefferson is basal, racial; the turn for academic philosophizing after the French fashion is personal, acquired; but the range and sweep and enduring vitality of this matchless state paper lie in its illumination of stubborn facts by general principles, its decent respect to the opinions of mankind, its stately and noble utterance of national sentiments and national reasons to a "candid world."

It has long been the fashion, among a certain school of half-hearted Americans — and unless I am mistaken, the teaching has increased during the last decades — to minimize the value of Jefferson's "self-evident truths." Rufus Choate, himself a consummate rhetorician, sneered at those "glittering generalities," and countless college-bred men, some of them occupying the highest positions, have echoed the sneer. The essence of the objection to Jefferson's platform lies of course in his phrase, "all men are created equal," with the subsidiary phrase about governments "deriving their just powers from the consent of the governed." Editors and congressmen and even college professors have proclaimed themselves unable to assent to these phrases of the Declaration, and unable even to understand them. These objectors belong partly, I think, in Jefferson's category of "nervous persons" — "anti-republicans," as he goes on to define them — "whose languid fibres have more analogy with a passive than an active state of things." Other objectors to the phrase "all men are created equal" have had an obvious personal or political motive for refusing assent to the proposition. But "no intelligent man," says one of Jefferson's biographers, "has ever misconstrued it [the Declaration] except intentionally."

Nobody would claim today that Thomas Jefferson's statement of the sentiments and reasons for the independence of the thirteen British colonies in 1776 was an adequate handbook of political wisdom, fit for all the exigencies of contemporary American democracy. It is not that. It is simply, in Lincoln's phrase, one of "the standard maxims of free society" which no democracy can safely disregard.

Jefferson's long life, so varied, so flexible, so responsive to the touch of popular forces, illustrates the process by which the Virginia mind of 1743 became the nationalized, unionized mind of 1826. It is needless here to dwell upon the traits of his personal character: his sweetness of spirit, his stout-heartedness in disaster, his scorn of money, his love for the intellectual life. "I have no ambition to govern men," he wrote to Edward Rutledge. He was far happier talking about Greek and Anglo-Saxon with Daniel Webster before the fire-place of Monticello than he ever was in the presidential chair. His correspondence was enormous. His writings fill twenty volumes. In his theories of education he was fifty years ahead of his time; in his absolute trust in humanity he was generations ahead of it. "I am not one of those who fear the people," he declared proudly. It is because of this touching faith, this invincible and matchless ardor, that Jefferson is today remembered. He foreshadowed Lincoln. His belief in the inarticulate common people is rewarded by their obstinate fidelity to his name as a type and symbol. "I know of no safe depository of the ultimate powers of society but the people themselves," wrote Jefferson, and with the people themselves is the depository of his fame.

CHAPTER V

THE Fourth of July orator for 1826 in Cambridge, Massachusetts, was Edward Everett. Although only thirty-two he was already a distinguished speaker. In the course of his oration he apostrophized John Adams and Thomas Jefferson as venerable survivors of that momentous day, fifty years earlier, which had witnessed our Declaration of Independence. But even as Everett was speaking, the aged author of the Declaration breathed his last at Monticello, and in the afternoon of that same day Adams died also, murmuring, it is said, with his latest breath, and as if with the whimsical obstinacy of an old man who hated to be beaten by his ancient rival, "Thomas Jefferson still lives." But Jefferson was already gone.

On the first of August, Everett commemorated the career of the two Revolutionary leaders, and on the following day a greater than Everett, Daniel

WILLIAM CULLEN BRYANT

Marble bust by Henry K. Brown.

EDWARD EVERETT

Plaster cast of bust by Clevenger.

JAMES FENIMORE COOPER

After a painting by J. W. Jarvis.

WASHINGTON IRVING

After a painting by C. R. Leslie.

Gravure Anderson-Lamb Co. NY

Webster, pronounced the famous eulogy in Faneuil Hall.   Never were the thoughts and emotions of a whole country more adequately voiced than in this commemorative oratory.   Its pulse was high with national pride over the accomplishments of half a century.   "I ask," Everett declared, "whether more has not been done to extend the domain of civilization, in fifty years, since the Declaration of Independence, than would have been done in five centuries of continued colonial subjection?"   Webster asserted in his peroration: "It cannot be denied, but by those who would dispute against the sun, that with America, and in America, a new era commences in human affairs.   This era is distinguished by free representative governments, by entire religious liberty, by improved systems of national intercourse, by a newly awakened and an unconquerable spirit of free enquiry, and by a diffusion of knowledge through the community such as has been before altogether unknown and unheard of."

Was this merely the "tall talk" then so characteristic of American oratory and soon to be satirized in *Martin Chuzzlewit?*   Or was it prompted by a deep and true instinct for the significance of the vast changes that had come over American life since 1776? The external changes were familiar enough to Webster's auditors: the opening of seemingly illimitable territory through the Louisiana Purchase, the development of roads, canals, and manufactures; a rapid increase in wealth and population; a shifting of political power due to the rise of the new West — in a word, the evidences of irrepressible national energy. But this energy was inadequately expressed by the national literature. The more cultivated Americans were quite aware of this deficiency. It was confessed by the pessimistic Fisher Ames and by the ardent young men who in 1815 founded *The North American Review*. British critics in *The Edinburgh* and *The Quarterly*, commenting upon recent works of travel in America, pointed out the literary poverty of the American soil. Sydney Smith, by no means the most offensive of these critics, declared in 1820: "During the thirty or forty years of their independence they have done absolutely nothing for the sciences, for the arts, for literature. . . . In the four quarters of the globe, who reads an American book? or goes to an American play? or looks at an American picture or statue?"

Sydney Smith's question "Who reads an American book?" has outlived all of his own clever volumes. Even while he was asking it, London was eagerly reading Irving's *Sketch Book*. In 1821 came Fenimore Cooper's *Spy* and Bryant's *Poems*, and by 1826, when Webster was announcing in his rolling orotund that Adams and Jefferson were no more, the London and Paris booksellers were covering their stalls with Cooper's *The Last of the Mohicans*. Irving, Cooper, and Bryant are thus the pioneers in a new phase of American literary activity, often called, for convenience in labeling, the Knickerbocker Group because of the identification of these men with New York. And close behind these leaders come a younger company, destined likewise, in the shy boyish words of Hawthorne, one of the number, "to write books that would be read in England." For by 1826 Hawthorne and Longfellow were out of college and were trying to learn to write. Ticknor, Prescott, and Bancroft, somewhat older men, were settling to their great tasks. Emerson was entering upon his duties as a minister. Edgar Allan Poe, at that University of Virginia which Jefferson had just founded, was doubtless revising *Tamerlane and Other Poems* which he was to publish in Boston in the following year. Holmes was a Harvard undergraduate. Garrison had just printed

Whittier's first published poem in the Newbury-port *Free Press*. Walt Whitman was a barefooted boy on Long Island, and Lowell, likewise seven years of age, was watching the birds in the tree-tops of Elmwood. But it was Washington Irving who showed all of these men that nineteenth century England would be interested in American books.

The very word Knickerbocker is one evidence of the vitality of Irving's happy imaginings. In 1809 he had invented a mythical Dutch historian of New York named Diedrich Knickerbocker and fathered upon him a witty parody of Dr. Mitchill's grave *Picture of New York*. To read Irving's chapters today is to witness one of the rarest and most agreeable of phenomena, namely, the actual beginning of a legend which the world is unwilling to let die. The book made Sir Walter Scott's sides ache with laughter, and reminded him of the humor of Swift and Sterne. But certain New Yorkers were slow to see the joke.

Irving was himself a New Yorker, born just at the close of the Revolution, of a Scotch father and English mother. His youth was pleasantly idle, with a little random education, much theater-going, and plentiful rambles with a gun along the

Hudson River. In 1804 he went abroad for his health, returned and helped to write the light social satire of the *Salmagundi Papers*, and became, after the publication of the *Knickerbocker History*, a local celebrity. Sailing for England in 1815 on business, he stayed until 1832 as a roving man of letters in England and Spain and then as Secretary of the American Legation in London. *The Sketch Book, Bracebridge Hall*, and *Tales of a Traveler* are the best known productions of Irving's fruitful residence in England. The *Life of Columbus*, the *Conquest of Granada*, and *The Alhambra* represent his first sojourn in Spain. After his return to America he became fascinated with the Great West, made the travels described in his *Tour of the Prairies*, and told the story of roving trappers and the fur trade in *Captain Bonneville* and *Astoria*. For four years he returned to Spain as American Minister. In his last tranquil years at Sunnyside on the Hudson, where he died in 1859, he wrote graceful lives of Goldsmith and of Washington.

Such a glance at the shelf containing Irving's books suggests but little of that personal quality to which he owes his significance as an interpreter of America to the Old World. This son of a narrow, hard, Scotch dealer in cutlery, this drifter

about town when New York was only a big slovenly village, this light-hearted scribbler of satire
and sentiment, was a gentleman born. His boyhood
and youth were passed in that period of Post-
Revolutionary reaction which exhibits the United
States in some of its most unlovely aspects.
Historians like Henry Adams and McMaster have
painted in detail the low estate of education, religion, and art as the new century began. The
bitter feeling of the nascent nation toward Great
Britain was intensified by the War of 1812. The
Napoleonic Wars had threatened to break the last
threads of our friendship for France, and suspicion
of the Holy Alliance led to an era of national self-
assertion of which the Monroe Doctrine was only
one expression. The raw Jacksonism of the West
seemed to be gaining upon the older civilizations
represented by Virginia and Massachusetts. The
self-made type of man began to pose as the genuine
American. And at this moment came forward a
man of natural lucidity and serenity of mind, of
perfect poise and good temper, who knew both
Europe and America and felt that they ought to
know one another better and to like one another
more. That was Irving's service as an international mediator. He diffused sweetness and

light in an era marked by bitterness and obscuration. It was a triumph of character as well as of literary skill.

But the skill was very noticeable also. Irving's prose is not that of the Defoe-Swift-Franklin-Paine type of plain talk to the crowd. It is rather an inheritance from that other eighteenth century tradition, the conversation of the select circle. Its accents were heard in Steele and Addison and were continued in Goldsmith, Sterne, Cowper, and Charles Lamb. Among Irving's successors, George William Curtis and Charles Dudley Warner and William Dean Howells have been masters of it likewise. It is mellow human talk, delicate, regardful, capable of exquisite modulation. With instinctive artistic taste, Irving used this old and sound style upon fresh American material. In *Rip van Winkle* and *The Legend of Sleepy Hollow* he portrayed his native valley of the Hudson, and for a hundred years connoisseurs of style have perceived the exquisite fitness of the language to the images and ideas which Irving desired to convey. To render the Far West of that epoch this style is perhaps not "big" and broad enough, but when used as Irving uses it in describing Stratford and Westminster Abbey and an Old English

Christmas, it becomes again a perfect medium. Hawthorne adopted it for *Our Old Home*, and Englishmen recognized it at once as a part of their own inheritance, enriched, like certain wines, by the voyage across the Atlantic and home again. Irving wrote of England, Mr. Warner once said, as Englishmen would have liked to write about it. When he described the Alhambra and Granada and the Moors, it was the style, rich both in physical sensation and in dreamlike reverie, which revealed to the world the quick American appreciation of foreign scenes and characters. Its key is sympathy.

Irving's popularity has endured in England. It suffered during the middle of the century in his own country, for the strongest New England authors taught the public to demand more thought and passion than were in Irving's nature. Possibly the nervous, journalistic style of the twentieth century allows too scanty leisure of mind for the full enjoyment of the Knickerbocker flavor. Yet such changes as these in literary fashion scarcely affect the permanent service of Irving to our literature. He immortalized a local type — the New York Dutchman — and local legends, like that of Rip van Winkle; he used the framework of the narrative essay to create something almost like the perfected short story of Poe and Hawthorne; he wrote prose with unfailing charm in an age when charm was lacking; and, if he had no message, it should be remembered that some of the most useful ambassadors have had none save to reveal, with delicacy and tact and humorous kindness, the truth that foreign persons have feelings precisely like our own.

Readers of Sir Walter Scott's *Journal* may remember his account of an evening party in Paris in 1826 where he met Fenimore Cooper, then in the height of his European reputation. "So the Scotch and American lions took the field together," wrote Sir Walter, who loved to be generous. *The Last of the Mohicans*, then just published, threatened to eclipse the fame of *Ivanhoe*. Cooper, born in 1789, was eighteen years younger than the Wizard of the North, and was more deeply indebted to him than he knew. For it was Scott who had created the immense nineteenth century audience for prose fiction, and who had evolved a kind of formula for the novel, ready for Cooper's use. Both men were natural story-tellers. Scott had the richer mind and the more fully developed historical imagination. Both were out-of-doors men, lovers of manly adventure and of natural beauty. But the American had the good fortune to be able to utilize in his books his personal experiences of forest and sea and to reveal to Europe the real romance of the American wilderness.

That Cooper was the first to perceive the artistic possibilities of this romance, no one would claim. Brockden Brown, a Quaker youth of Philadelphia, a disciple of the English Godwin, had tried his hand at the very end of the eighteenth century upon American variations of the Gothic romance then popular in England. Brown had a keen eye for the values of the American landscape and even of the American Indian. He had a knack for passages of ghastly power, as his descriptions of maniacs, murderers, sleep-walkers, and solitaries abundantly prove. But he had read too much and lived too little to rival the masters of the art of fiction. And there was a traveled Frenchman, Chateaubriand, surely an expert in the art of eloquent prose, who had transferred to the pages of his American Indian stories, *Atala* and *René*, the mystery and enchantment of our dark forests and endless rivers. But Chateaubriand, like Brockden Brown, is feverish. A taint of old-world eroticism and despair hovers like a miasma over his magnificent panorama of the wilderness.   Cooper, like Scott, is masculine.

He was a Knickerbocker only by adoption. Born in New Jersey, his childhood was spent in the then remote settlement of Cooperstown in Central New York.   He had a little schooling at Albany, and a brief and inglorious career at Yale with the class of 1806.   He went to sea for two years, and then served for three years in the United States Navy upon Lakes Ontario and Champlain, the very scene of some of his best stories.   In 1811 he married, resigned from the Navy, and settled upon a little estate in Westchester County, near New York.   Until the age of thirty, he was not in the least a bookman, but a healthy man of action. Then, as the well-known anecdote goes, he exclaims to his wife, after reading a stupid English novel, "I believe I could write a better story myself." *Precaution* (1820) was the result, but whether it was better than the unknown English book, no one can now say.   It was bad enough.   Yet the next year Cooper published *The Spy*, one of the finest of his novels, which was instantly welcomed in England and translated in France.   Then came, in swift succession, *The Pioneers*, the first Leather-

7

Stocking tale in order of composition, and *The Pilot*, to show that Scott's *Pirate* was written by a landsman! *Lionel Lincoln* and *The Last of the Mohicans* followed. The next seven years were spent in Europe, mainly in France, where *The Prairie* and *The Red Rover* were written. Cooper now looked back upon his countrymen with eyes of critical detachment, and made ready to tell them some of their faults. He came home to Cooperstown in 1833, the year after Irving's return to America. He had won, deservedly, a great fame, which he proceeded to imperil by his combativeness with his neighbors and his harsh strictures upon the national character, due mainly to his lofty conception of the ideal America. He continued to spin yarns of sea and shore, and to write naval history. The tide of fashion set against him in the eighteen-forties when Bulwer and Dickens rode into favor, but the stouthearted old pioneer could afford to bide his time. He died in 1851, just as Mrs. Stowe was writing *Uncle Tom's Cabin*.

Two generations have passed since then, and Cooper's place in our literature remains secure. To have written our first historical novel, *The Spy*, our first sea-story, *The Pilot*, and to have created the Leather-Stocking series, is glory enough. In his perception of masculine character, Cooper ranks with Fielding. His sailors, his scouts and spies, his good and bad Indians, are as veritable human figures as Squire Western. Long Tom Coffin, Harvey Birch, Hawk-Eye, and Chingachgook are physically and morally true to life itself. Read the Leather-Stocking books in the order of the events described, beginning with *The Deerslayer*, then *The Last of the Mohicans*, *The Pathfinder*, *The Pioneers*, and ending with the vast darkening horizon of *The Prairie* and the death of the trapper, and one will feel how natural and inevitable are the fates of the personages and the alterations in the life of the frontier. These books vary in their poetic quality and in the degree of their realism, but to watch the evolution of the leading figure is to see human life in its actual texture.

Clever persons and pedantic persons have united to find fault with certain elements of Cooper's art. Mark Twain, in one of his least inspired moments, selected Cooper's novels for attack. Every grammar school teacher is ready to point out that his style is often prolix and his sentences are sometimes ungrammatical. Amateurs even criticize Cooper's seamanship, although it seemed impeccable to Admiral Mahan. No doubt one must admit the "helplessness, propriety, and incapacity" of most of Cooper's women, and the dreadfulness of his bores, particularly the Scotchmen, the doctors, and the naturalists. Like Sir Walter, Cooper seems to have taken but little pains in the deliberate planning of his plots. Frequently he accepts a ready-made formula of villain and hero, predicament and escape, renewed crisis and rescue, mystification and explanation, worthy of a third-rate novelist. His salvation lies in his genius for action, the beauty and grandeur of his landscapes, the primitive veracity of his children of nature.

Cooper was an elemental man, and he comprehended, by means of something deeper than mere artistic instinct, the feelings of elemental humanity in the presence of the wide ocean or of the deep woods. He is as healthy and sane as Fielding, and he possesses an additional quality which all of the purely English novelists lack. It was the result of his youthful sojourn in the wilderness. Let us call it the survival in him of an aboriginal imagination. Cooper reminds one somehow of a moose — an ungraceful creature perhaps, but indubitably big, as many a hunter has suddenly realized when he has come unexpectedly upon a moose that whirled to face him in the twilight silence of a northern wood.

Something of this far-off and gigantic primitivism inheres also in the poetry of William Cullen Bryant. His portrait, with the sweeping white beard and the dark folds of the cloak, suggests the Bard as the Druids might have known him. But in the eighteen-thirties and forties, Mr. Bryant's alert, clean-shaven face, and energetic gait as he strode down Broadway to the *Evening Post* office, suggested little more than a vigorous and somewhat radical editor of an increasingly prosperous Democratic newspaper. There was nothing of the Fringed Gentian or Yellow Violet about him. Like so many of the Knickerbockers, Bryant was an immigrant to New York; in fact, none of her adopted men of letters have represented so perfectly the inherited traits of the New England Puritan. To understand his long and honorable public life it is necessary to know something of the city of his choice, but to enter into the spirit of his poetry one must go back to the hills of western Massachusetts.

Bryant had a right to his cold-weather mind. He came from Mayflower stock. His father, Dr.

Peter Bryant of Cummington, was a sound country physician, with liberal preferences in theology,
Federalist views in politics, and a library of seven
hundred volumes, rich in poetry. The poet's
mother records his birth in her diary in terse words
which have the true Spartan tang: "Nov. 3, 1794.
Stormy, wind N. E. Churned. Seven in the
evening a son born." Two days later the November wind shifted. "Nov. 5, 1794. Clear, wind
N. W. Made Austin a coat. Sat up all day.
Went into the kitchen." The baby, it appears,
had an abnormally large head and was dipped,
day after day, in rude hydropathy, into an icy
spring. A precocious childhood was followed by a
stern, somewhat unhappy, but aspiring boyhood.
The little fellow, lying prone with his brothers
before the firelight of the kitchen, reading English
poetry from his father's library, used to pray that
he too might become a poet. At thirteen he produced a satire on Jefferson, *The Embargo*, which his
proud Federalist father printed at Boston in 1808.
The youth had nearly one year at Williams College, over the mountain ranges to the west. He
wished to continue his education at Yale, but his
father had no money for this greater venture, and
the son remained at home. There, in the autumn

of 1811, on the bleak hills, he composed the first draft of *Thanatopsis*. He was seventeen, and he had been reading Blair's *Grave* and the poems of the consumptive Henry Kirke White. He hid his verses in a drawer, and five years later his father found them, shed tears over them, and sent them to the *North American Review*, where they were published in September, 1817.

In the meantime the young man had studied law, though with dislike of it, and with the confession that he sometimes read *The Lyrical Ballads* when he might have been reading Blackstone. One December afternoon in 1815, he was walking from Cummington to Plainfield — aged twenty-one, and looking for a place in which to settle as a lawyer. Across the vivid sunset flew a black duck, as solitary and homeless as himself. The bird seemed an image of his own soul, "lone wandering but not lost." Before he slept that night he had composed the poem *To a Waterfowl*. No more authentic inspiration ever visited a poet, and though Bryant wrote verse for more than sixty years after that crimson sky had paled into chill December twilight, his lines never again vibrated with such communicative passion.

Bryant's ensuing career revealed the steady purpose, the stoicism, the reticence of the Puritan. It was highly successful, judged even by material standards. *Thanatopsis* had been instantly regarded in 1817 as the finest poem yet produced in America. The author was invited to contribute to the *North American Review* an essay on American poetry, and this, like all of Bryant's prose work, was admirably written. He delivered his Harvard Phi Beta Kappa poem, *The Ages*, in 1821, the year of Emerson's graduation. After a brief practice of the law in Great Barrington, he entered in 1826 into the unpromising field of journalism in New York. While other young Knickerbockers wasted their literary strength on trifles and dissipated their moral energies, Bryant held steadily to his daily task. His life in town was sternly ascetic, but he allowed himself long walks in the country, and he continued to meditate a somewhat thankless Muse. In 1832 he visited his brothers on the Illinois prairies, and stopped one day to chat with a "tall awkward uncouth lad" of racy conversational powers, who was leading his company of volunteers into the Black Hawk War. The two men were destined to meet again in 1860, when Bryant presided at that Cooper Union address of Lincoln's which revealed to New York and to the country that the former captain of volunteers was now a king of men. Lincoln was embarrassed on that occasion, it is said, by Bryant's fastidious, dignified presence. Not so Nathaniel Hawthorne, who had seen the poet in Rome, two years before. "There was a weary look in his face," wrote Hawthorne, "as if he were tired of seeing things and doing things. . . . He uttered neither passion nor poetry, but excellent good sense, and accurate information, on whatever subject transpired; a very pleasant man to associate with, but rather cold, I should imagine, if one should seek to touch his heart with one's own." Such was the impression Bryant made upon less gifted men than Hawthorne, as he lived out his long and useful life in the Knicker-bocker city. Toward the close of it he was in great demand for public occasions; and it was after delivering a speech dedicating a statue to Mazzini in Central Park in 1878, when Bryant was eighty-four, that a fit of dizziness caused a fall which proved fatal to the venerable poet. It was just seventy years since Dr. Peter Bryant had published his boy's verses on *The Embargo*.

Although Bryant's poetry has never roused any vociferous excitement, it has enduring qualities. The spiritual preoccupations of many a voiceless generation of New England Puritans found a tongue at last in this late-born son of theirs. The determining mood of his best poems, from boyhood to old age, was precisely that thought of transiency, "the eternal flow of things," which colored the imaginations of the first colonists. This is the central motive of *Thanatopsis, To a Waterfowl, The Rivulet, A Forest Hymn, An Evening Revery, The Crowded Street, The Flood of Years*. All of these tell the same story of endless change and of endless abiding, of varying eddies in the same mighty stream of human existence. Bryant faced the thought as calmly, as majestically, at seventeen as when he wrote *The Flood of Years* at eighty-two. He is a master of description, though he has slight gift for narrative or drama, and he rarely sounds the clear lyric note. But everywhere in his verse there is that cold purity of the winter hills in Western Massachusetts, something austere and elemental which reaches kindred spirits below the surface on which intellect and passion have their play, something more primitive, indeed, than human intellect or passion and belonging to another mode of being, something "rock-ribbed and ancient as the sun."

A picture of the Knickerbocker era is not complete without its portraits of the minor figures in the literary life of New York up to the time of the Civil War. But the scope of the present volume does not permit sketches of Paulding and Verplanck, of Halleck and his friend Drake, of N. P. Willis and Morris and Woodworth. Some of these are today only "single-poem" men, like Payne, the author of *Home Sweet Home*, just as Key, the author of *The Star-Spangled Banner*, is today a "single-poem" man of an earlier generation. Their names will be found in such limbos of the dead as Griswold's *Poets and Poetry of America* and Poe's *Literati*. They knew "the town" in their day, and pleased its very easily pleased taste. The short-lived literary magazines of the eighteen-forties gave them their hour of glory. As representatives of passing phases of the literary history of New York their careers are not without sentimental interest, but few of them spoke to or for the country as a whole. Two figures, indeed, stand out in sharp contrast with those habitual strollers on Broadway and frequenters of literary gatherings, though each of them was for a while a part of Knickerbocker New York. To all appearances they were only two more Bohemians like the rest, but the curiosity of the twentieth

century sets them apart from their forgotten contemporaries. They are two of the unluckiest —
and yet luckiest — authors who ever tried to sell
a manuscript along Broadway. One of them is
Edgar Allan Poe and the other is Walt Whitman.
They shall have a chapter to themselves.

But before turning to that chapter, we must
look back to New England once more and observe
the blossoming-time of its ancient commonwealths.
During the thirty years preceding the Civil War
New England awoke to a new life of the spirit.
So varied and rich was her literary productiveness
in this era that it still remains her greatest period,
and so completely did New England writers of this
epoch voice the ideals of the nation that the great
majority of Americans, even today, regard these
New Englanders as the truest literary exponents
of the mind and soul of the United States. We
must take a look at them.

CHAPTER VI

THE TRANSCENDENTALISTS

To understand the literary leadership of New England during the thirty years immediately preceding the Civil War it is necessary to recall the characteristics of a somewhat isolated and peculiar people. The mental and moral traits of the New England colonists, already glanced at in an earlier chapter, had suffered little essential modification in two hundred years. The original racial stock was still dominant. As compared with the middle and southern colonies, there was relatively little immigration, and this was easily assimilated. The physical remoteness of New England from other sections of the country, and the stubborn loyalty with which its inhabitants maintained their own standards of life, alike contributed to their sense of separateness. It is true, of course, that their mode of thinking and feeling had undergone certain changes. They were among the earliest theorists, of political independence from Great Britain, and had done their share, and more, in the Revolution. The rigors of their early creed had somewhat relaxed, as we have seen, by the end of the seventeenth century, and throughout the eighteenth there was a gradual progress toward religious liberalism. The population steadily increased, and New England's unremitting struggle with a not too friendly soil, her hardihood upon the seas, and her keenness in trade, became proverbial throughout the country. Her seaport towns were wealthy. The general standards of living remained frugal, but extreme poverty was rare. Her people still made, as in the earliest days of the colonies, silent and unquestioned sacrifices for education, and her chief seats of learning, Harvard and Yale, remained the foremost educational centers of America. But there was still scant leisure for the quest of beauty, and slender material reward for any practitioner of the fine arts. Oratory alone, among the arts of expression, commanded popular interest and applause. Daniel Webster's audiences at Plymouth in 1820 and at Bunker Hill in 1825 were not inferior to similar audiences of today in intelligence and in responsiveness. Perhaps they were superior. Appreci-

ation of the spoken word was natural to men
trained by generations of thoughtful listening to
"painful" preaching and by participation in the
discussions of town-meeting. Yet appreciation
of secular literature was rare, and interest in the
other arts was almost non-existent.

Then, beginning in the eighteen-twenties, and
developing rapidly after 1830, came a change, a
change so startling as to warrant the term of "the
Renascence of New England." No single cause is
sufficient to account for this "new birth." It is a
good illustration of that law of "tension and release," which the late Professor Shaler liked to
demonstrate in all organic life. A long period of
strain was followed by an age of expansion, freedom, release of energy. As far as the mental life
of New England was concerned, something of the
new stimulus was due directly to the influence of
Europe. Just as the wandering scholars from
Italy had brought the New Learning, which was a
revival of the old learning, into England in the
sixteenth century, so now young New England
college men like Edward Everett and George Ticknor brought home from the Continent the riches
of German and French scholarship. Emerson's
description of the impression made by Everett's

lectures in 1820, after his return from Germany, gives a vivid picture of the new thirst for foreign culture. *The North American Review* and other periodicals, while persistently urging the need of a distinctively national literature, insisted also upon the value of a deeper knowledge of the literature of the Continent. This was the burden of Channing's once famous article on *A National Literature* in 1823: it was a plea for an independent American school of writers, but these writers should know the best that Europe had to teach.

The purely literary movement was connected, as the great name of Channing suggests, with a new sense of freedom in philosophy and religion. Calvinism had mainly done its work in New England. It had bred an extraordinary type of men and women, it had helped to lay some of the permanent foundations of our democracy, and it was still destined to have a long life in the new West and in the South. But in that stern section of the country where its influence had been most marked there was now an increasingly sharp reaction against its determinism and its pessimism. Early in the nineteenth century the most ancient and influential churches in Boston and the leading professors at Harvard had accepted the new form of religious liberalism known as Unitarianism. The movement spread throughout Eastern Massachusetts and made its way to other States. Orthodox and liberal Congregational churches split apart, and when Channing preached the ordination sermon for Jared Sparks in Baltimore in 1819, the word Unitarian, accepted by the liberals with some misgiving, became the recognized motto of the new creed. It is only with its literary influence that we are here concerned, yet that literary influence became so potent that there is scarcely a New England writer of the first rank, from Bryant onward, who remained untouched by it.

The most interesting and peculiar phase of the new liberalism has little directly to do with the specific tenets of theological Unitarianism, and in fact marked a revolt against the more prosaic and conventional pattern of English and American Unitarian thought. But this movement, known as Transcendentalism, would have been impossible without a preliminary and liberalizing stirring of the soil. It was a fascinating moment of release for some of the most brilliant and radical minds of New England. Its foremost representative in our literature was Ralph Waldo Emerson, as its chief

8

exponents in England were Coleridge and Carlyle. We must understand its meaning if we would perceive the quality of much of the most noble and beautiful writing produced in New England during the Golden Age.

What then is the significance of the word Transcendental? Disregarding for the moment the technical development of this term as used by German and English philosophers, it meant for Emerson and his friends simply this: whatever transcends or goes beyond the experience of the senses. It stressed intuition rather than sensation, direct perception of ultimate truth rather than the processes of logic. It believed in man's ability to apprehend the absolute ideas of Truth, Rectitude, Goodness. It resembled the Inner Light of the Quaker, though the Quaker traced this to a supernatural illumination of the Holy Spirit, while the Transcendentalist believed that a vision of the eternal realities was a natural endowment of the human mind. It had only to be trusted. Stated in this form, it is evident that we have here a very ancient doctrine, well known in the literature of India and of Greece. It has been held by countless persons who have never heard of the word Transcendentalism. We need go no further back than Alexander Pope, a Roman Catholic, whom we find declaring: "I am so certain of the soul's being immortal that I seem to feel it within me, as it were by intuition." Pope's friend Swift, a dean of the Church of England and assuredly no Transcendentalist, defined vision as seeing the things that are invisible.

Now turn to some of the New England men. Dr. C. A. Bartol, a disciple of Emerson, maintained that "the mistake is to make the everlasting things subjects of argument instead of sight." Theodore Parker declared to his congregation:

From the primitive facts of consciousness given by the power of instinctive intuition, I endeavored to deduce the true notion of God, of justice and futurity. . . . I found most help in the works of Immanuel Kant, one of the profoundest thinkers of the world, though one of the worst writers, even in Germany; if he did not always furnish conclusions I could rest in, he yet gave me the true method, and put me on the right road. I found certain great primal Intuitions of Human Nature, which depend on no logical process of demonstration, but are rather facts of consciousness given by the instinctive action of human nature itself. I will mention only the three most important which pertain to Religion. 1. The Instinctive Intuition of the Divine, the consciousness that there is a God. 2. The Instinctive Intuition of the Just and Right, a consciousness that there is a Moral Law, independent of our will, which we ought to keep. 3. The Instinctive Intuition of the Immortal, a consciousness that the Essential Element of man, the principle of Individuality, never dies.

This passage dates from 1859, and readers of Bergson may like to compare it with the contemporary Frenchman's saying: "The analytical faculties can give us no realities."

Let us next hear Emerson himself, first in an early letter to his brother Edward: "Do you draw the distinction of Milton, Coleridge, and the Germans between Reason and Understanding? I think it a philosophy itself, and, like all truth, very practical. Reason is the highest faculty of the soul, what we mean often by the soul itself: it never reasons, never proves, it simply perceives, it is vision. The understanding toils all the time, compares, contrives, adds, argues; near-sighted, but strong-sighted, dwelling in the present, the expedient, the customary." And in 1833, after he had left the Unitarian pulpit, Emerson made in his diary this curious attempt to reconcile the scriptural language of his ancestral profession to the new vocabulary of Transcendentalism: "Jesus Christ was a minister of the pure Reason. The beatitudes of the Sermon on the Mount are all utterances of the

mind contemning the phenomenal world. . . .
The understanding can make nothing of it. 'Tis
all nonsense. The Reason affirms its absolute
verity. . . . St. Paul marks the distinction
by the terms natural man and spiritual man.
When Novalis says, 'It is the instinct of the Understanding to contradict the Reason,' he only
translates into a scientific formula the doctrine of
St. Paul, 'The Carnal Mind is enmity against
God.'"

One more quotation must suffice. It is from a
poem by a forgotten Transcendentalist, F. G.
Tuckerman.

No more thy meaning seek, thine anguish plead;
But, leaving straining thought and stammering word,
Across the barren azure pass to God;
Shooting the void in silence, like a bird—
A bird that shuts his wings for better speed!

It is obvious that this "contemning the phenomenal world," this "revulsion against the
intellect as the sole source of truth," is highly dangerous to second-class minds. If one habitually
prints the words Insight, Instinct, Intuition, Consciousness with capitals, and relegates equally
useful words like senses, experience, fact, logic to
lower-case type, one may do it because he is a

Carlyle or an Emerson, but the chances are that he is neither. Transcendentalism, like all idealistic movements, had its "lunatic fringe," its camp-followers of excitable, unstable visionaries. The very name, like the name Methodist, was probably bestowed upon it in mockery, and this whole perturbation of staid New England had its humorous side. Witness the career of Bronson Alcott. It is also true that the glorious affirmations of these seers can be neither proved nor disproved. They made no examination and they sought no validation of consciousness. An explorer in search of the North Pole must bring back proofs of his journey, but when a Transcendentalist affirms that he has reached the far heights of human experience and even caught sight of the gods sitting on their thrones, you and I are obliged to take his word for it. Sometimes we hear such a man gladly, but it depends upon the man, not upon the trustworthiness of the method. Finally it should be observed that the Transcendental movement was an exceedingly complex one, being both literary, philosophic, and religious; related also to the subtle thought of the Orient, to mediæval mysticism, and to the English Platonists; touched throughout by the French Revolu-

RALPH WALDO EMERSON

Photograph by Black, Boston.

RALPH WALDO EMERSON

Photograph by Black, Boston.

tionary theories, by the Romantic spirit, by the new zeal for science and pseudo-science, and by the unrest of a fermenting age.

Our present concern is with the impact of this cosmopolitan current upon the mind and character of a few New England writers. Channing and Theodore Parker, Margaret Fuller and Alcott, Thoreau and Emerson, are all representative of the best thought and the noblest ethical impulses of their generation. Let us choose first the greatest name: a sunward-gazing spirit, and, it may be, one of the very Sun-Gods.

The pilgrim to Concord who stops for a moment in the village library to study French's statue of Emerson will notice the asymmetrical face. On one side it is the face of a keen Yankee farmer, but seen from the other side it is the countenance of a seer, a world's man. This contrast between the parochial Emerson and the greater Emerson interprets many a puzzle in his career. Half a mile beyond the village green to the north, close to the "rude bridge" of the famous Concord fight in 1775, is the Old Manse, once tenanted and described by Hawthorne. It was built by Emerson's grandfather, a patriot chaplain in the Revolution, who died of camp-fever at Ticonderoga. His widow married Dr. Ezra Ripley, and here Ralph Waldo Emerson and his brothers passed many a summer in their childhood. Half a mile east of the village, on the Cambridge turnpike, is Emerson's own house, still sheltered by the pines which Thoreau helped him to plant in 1838. Within the house everything is unchanged: here are the worn books, pen and inkstand, the favorite pictures upon the wall. Over the ridge to the north lies the Sleepy Hollow cemetery where the poet rests, with the gravestones of Hawthorne and the Alcotts, Thoreau and William James close by.

But although Concord is the Emerson shrine, he was born in Boston, in 1803. His father, named William like the grandfather, was also, like the Emerson ancestors for many generations, a clergyman — eloquent, liberal, fond of books and music, highly honored by his *alma mater* Harvard and by the town of Boston, where he ministered to the First Church. His premature death in 1811 left his widow with five sons — one of them feebleminded — and a daughter to struggle hard with poverty. With her husband's sister, the Calvinistic "Aunt Mary Moody" Emerson, she held, however, that these orphaned boys had been "born to be educated." And educated the "eager blushing boys" were, at the Boston Latin School and at Harvard College, on a regimen of "toil and want and truth and mutual faith." There are many worse systems of pedagogy than this. Ralph was thought less persistent than his steady older brother William, and far less brilliant than his gifted, short-lived younger brothers, Edward and Charles. He had an undistinguished career at Harvard, where he was graduated in 1821, ranking thirtieth in a class of fifty-nine. Lovers of irony like to remember that he was the seventh choice of his classmates for the position of class poet. After some desultory teaching to help his brothers, he passed irregularly through the Divinity School, his studies often interrupted by serious ill-health. "If they had examined me," he said afterward of the kindly professors in the Divinity School, "they never would have passed me." But approve him they did, in 1826, and he entered decorously upon the profession of his ancestors, as associate minister of the Second Church in Boston. His *Journals*, which are a priceless record of his inner life, at this and later periods, reveal the rigid self-scrutiny, the tender idealism, with which he began his ministerial career.

But as a scheme of life for Ralph Waldo Emerson this vocation would not satisfy. The sexton of the Second Church thought that the young man was not at his best at funerals. Father Taylor, the eccentric Methodist, whom Emerson assisted at a sailor's Bethel near Long Wharf, considered him "one of the sweetest souls God ever made," but as ignorant of the principles of the New Testament as Balaam's ass was of Hebrew grammar. By and by came an open difference with his congregation over the question of administering the Communion. "I am not interested in it," Emerson admitted, and he wrote in his *Journal* the noble words: "It is my desire, in the office of a Christian minister, to do nothing which I cannot do with my whole heart." His resignation was accepted in 1832. His young wife had died of consumption in the same year. He now sailed for Italy, France, and England, a memorable journey which gave him an acquaintance with Landor, Wordsworth, Coleridge, and Carlyle, but which was even more significant in sending him, as he says, back to himself, to the resources of his own nature. "When shows break up," wrote Whitman afterward, "what but oneself is sure?" In 1834 and 1835 we find Emerson occupying a room in the Old Manse at Concord, strolling in the quiet fields, lecturing or preaching if he were invited to do so, but chiefly absorbed in a little book which he was beginning to write — a new utterance of a new man.

This book, the now famous *Nature* of 1836, contains the essence of Emerson's message to his generation. It is a prose essay, but written in the ecstatic mood of a poet. The theme of its meditation is the soul as related to Nature and to God. The soul is primal; Nature, in all its bountiful and beautiful commodities, exists for the training of the soul; it is the soul's shadow. And every soul has immediate access to Deity. Thus the utility and beauty and discipline of Nature lift the soul Godward. The typical sentence of the book is this: "The sun shines today also"; that is to say: the world is still alive and fair; let us lift up our hearts! Only a few Americans of 1836 bought this singular volume, but Emerson went serenely forward. He had found his path.

In 1837 he delivered the well-known Phi Beta Kappa oration at Harvard on *The American Scholar*. Emerson was now thirty-four; he had married a second time, had bought a house of his own in Concord, and purposed to make a living by lecturing and writing. His address in Cambridge, though it contained no reference to himself, was after all a justification of the way of life he had chosen: a declaration of intellectual independence for himself and his countrymen, an exhortation of self-trust to the individual thinking man. "If the single man plant himself indomitably on his instincts and there abide, the huge world will come round to him." Such advice to cut loose from the moorings of the past was not unknown in Phi Beta Kappa orations, though it had never been so brilliantly phrased; but when Emerson applied precisely the same doctrine, in 1838, to the graduating class at the Harvard Divinity School, he roused a storm of disapproval. "A tempest in our washbowl," he wrote coolly to Carlyle, but it was more than that. The great sentence of the Divinity School address, "God is, not was; he speaketh, not spake," was the emphasis of a superb rhetorician upon the immediacy of the soul's access to God. It has been the burden of a thousand prophets in all religions. The young priests of the Divinity School, their eyes wearied with Hebrew and Greek, seem to have enjoyed Emerson's injunction to turn away from past records and historical authorities and to drink from the living fountain of the divine within themselves; but to the professors, "the stern old war-gods," this relative belittlement of historical Christianity seemed blasphemy. A generation passed before Emerson was again welcomed by his *alma mater*.

The reader who has mastered those three utterances by the Concord Transcendentalist in 1836, 1837, and 1838 has the key to Emerson. He was a seer, not a system-maker. The constitution of his mind forbade formal, consecutive, logical thought. He was not a philosopher in the accepted sense, though he was always philosophizing, nor a metaphysician in spite of his curious searchings in the realm of metaphysics. He sauntered in books as he sauntered by Walden Pond, in quest of what interested him; he "fished in Montaigne," he said, as he fished in Plato and Goethe. He basketed the day's luck, good or bad as it might be, into the pages of his private *Journal*, which he called his savings-bank, because from this source he drew most of the material for his books. The *Journal* has recently been printed, in ten volumes. No American writing rewards the reader more richly. It must be remembered that Emerson's *Essays*, the first volume of which appeared in 1841, and the last volumes after his death in 1882, represent practically three stages of composition: first the detached thoughts of the *Journal;* second, the rearrangement of this material for use upon the lecture platform; and finally, the essays in their present form. The oral method thus predominates: a series of oracular thoughts has been shaped for oratorical utterance, not oratorical in the bombastic, popular American sense, but cunningly designed, by a master of rhetoric, to capture the ear and then the mind of the auditor.

Emerson's work as a lecturer coincided with the rise of that Lyceum system which brought most of the American authors, for more than a generation, into intimate contact with the public, and which proved an important factor in the æsthetic and moral cultivation of our people. No lecturer could have had a more auspicious influence than Emerson, with his quiet dignity, his serene spiritual presence, his tonic and often electrifying force. But if he gave his audiences precious gifts, he also learned much from them. For thirty years his lecturing trips to the West brought him, more widely than any New England man of letters, into contact with the new, virile America of the great Mississippi valley. Unlike many of his friends, he was not repelled by the "Jacksonism of the West"; he rated it a wholesome, vivifying force in our national thought and life. The *Journal* reveals the essential soundness of his Americanism. Though surrounded all his life by reformers, he was himself scarcely a reformer, save upon the single issue of anti-slavery. Perhaps he was at bottom too much of a radical to be swept off his feet by any reform.

To our generation, of course, Emerson presents himself as an author of books, and primarily as an essayist, rather than as a winning, entrancing speaker. His essays have a greater variety of tone than is commonly recognized. Many of them, like *Manners*, *Farming*, *Books*, *Eloquence*, *Old Age*, exhibit a shrewd prudential wisdom, a sort of Yankee instinct for "the milk in the pan," that reminds one of Ben Franklin. Like most of the greater New England writers, he could be, on occasion, an admirable local historian. See his essays on *Life and Letters in New England*, *New England Reformers*, *Politics*, and the successive entries in his *Journal* relating to Daniel Webster. He had the happiest gift of portraiture, as is witnessed by his sketches of Montaigne, of Napoleon, of Socrates (in the essay on Plato), of his aunt Mary Moody Emerson, of Thoreau, and of various types of

Englishmen in his *English Traits*. But the great essays, no doubt, are those like *Self-Reliance, Compensation, The Over-Soul, Fate, Power, Culture, Worship,* and *Illusions.* These will puzzle no one who has read carefully that first book on *Nature.* They all preach the gospel of intuition, instinctive trust in the Universe, faith in the ecstatic moment of vision into the things that are unseen by the physical eye. Self-reliance, as Emerson's son has pointed out, means really God-reliance; the Over-Soul — always a stumbling-block to Philistines — means that high spiritual life into which all men may enter and in which they share the life of Deity. Emerson is stern enough in expounding the laws of compensation that run through the universe, but to him the chief law is the law of the ever-ascending, victorious soul.

This radiant optimism permeates his poems. By temperament a singer as well as a seer and sayer, Emerson was nevertheless deficient in the singing voice. He composed no one great poem, his verse presents no ideas that are not found in his prose. In metre and rhyme he is harsh and willful. Yet he has marvelous single phrases and cadences. He ejaculates transports and ecstasies, and though he cannot organize and construct in verse, he is

capable here and there of the true miracle of
transforming fact and thought into true beauty.
Aldrich used to say that he would rather have
written Emerson's *Bacchus* than any American
poem.

That the pure, high, and tonic mind of Emerson
was universal in its survey of human forces, no
one would claim.   Certain limitations in interest
and sympathy are obvious.   "That horrid burden
and impediment of the soul which the churches call
sin," to use John Morley's words, occupied his
attention but little.   Like a mountain climber in a
perilous pass, he preferred to look up rather than
down.   He does not stress particularly those old
human words, service and sacrifice.   "Anti-scien-
tific, anti-social, anti-Christian" are the terms applied to him by one of his most penetrating critics.
Yet I should prefer to say "un-scientific," "un-
social," and "non-Christian," in the sense in which
Plato and Isaiah are non-Christian.   Perhaps it
would be still nearer the truth to say, as Mrs.
Lincoln said of her husband, "He was not a technical Christian."   He tends to underestimate
institutions of every kind; history, except as a storehouse of anecdote, and culture as a steady mental
discipline.   This is the price he pays for his tran-

9

scendental insistence upon the supreme value of the Now, the moment of insight. But after all these limitations are properly set down, the personality of Ralph Waldo Emerson remains a priceless possession to his countrymen. The austere serenity of his life, and the perfection with which he represents the highest type of his province and his era, will ultimately become blended with the thought of his true Americanism. A democrat and liberator, like Lincoln, he seems also destined like Lincoln to become increasingly a world's figure, a friend and guide to aspiring spirits everywhere. Differences of race and creed are negligible in the presence of such superb confidence in God and the soul.

Citizens of Concord in May, 1862, hearing that Henry Thoreau, the eccentric bachelor, had just died of consumption in his mother's house on Main Street, in his forty-fifth year, would have smiled cannily at the notion that after fifty years their townsman's literary works would be published in a sumptuous twenty-volume edition, and that critics in his own country and in Europe would rank him with Ralph Waldo Emerson. Yet that is precisely what has happened. Our literature has no more curious story than the evolution of this local crank

into his rightful place of mastership.   In his lifetime he printed only two books, *A Week on the
Concord and Merrimac Rivers* — which was even
more completely neglected by the public than
Emerson's *Nature* — and *Walden*, now one of the
classics, but only beginning to be talked about
when its shy, proud author penned his last line
and died with the words "moose" and "Indian"
on his lips.

Thoreau, like all thinkers who reach below the
surface of human life, means many different things
to men of various temperaments.   Collectors of human novelties, like Stevenson, rejoice in his unique-
ness of flavor; critics, like Lowell, place him, not
without impatient rigor.   To some readers he is
primarily a naturalist, an observer, of the White
of Selborne school; to others an elemental man, a
lover of the wild, a hermit of the woods.   He has
been called the poet-naturalist, to indicate that his
powers of observation were accompanied, like
Wordsworth's, by a gift of emotional interpretation of the meaning of phenomena.   Lovers of
literature celebrate his sheer force and penetration
of phrase.   But to the student of American
thought Thoreau's prime value lies in the courage
and consistency with which he endeavored to

realize the gospel of Transcendentalism in his own inner life.

Lovers of racial traits like to remember that Thoreau's grandfather was an immigrant Frenchman from the island of Jersey, and that his grandmother was Scotch and Quaker. His father made lead pencils and ground plumbago in his own house in Concord. The mother was from New Hampshire. It was a high-minded family. All the four children taught school and were good talkers. Henry, born in 1817, was duly baptized by good Dr. Ripley of the Old Manse, studied Greek and Latin, and was graduated at Harvard in 1837, the year of Emerson's Phi Beta Kappa address. Even in college the young man was a trifle difficult. "Cold and unimpressible," wrote a classmate. "The touch of his hand was moist and indifferent. He did not care for people." "An unfavorable opinion has been entertained of his disposition to exert himself," wrote President Quincy confidentially to Emerson in 1837, although the kindly President, a year later, in recommending Thoreau as a school-teacher, certified that "his rank was high as a scholar in all the branches and his morals and general conduct unexceptionable and exemplary."

Ten years passed. The young man gave up

school-keeping, thinking it a loss of time. He learned pencil-making, surveying, and farm work, and found that by manual labor for six weeks in the year he could meet all the expenses of living. He haunted the woods and pastures, explored rivers and ponds, built the famous hut on Emerson's wood-lot with the famous axe borrowed from Alcott, was put in jail for refusal to pay his poll-tax, and, to sum up much in little, "signed off" from social obligations. "I, Henry D. Thoreau, have signed off, and do not hold myself responsible to your multifarious uncivil chaos named Civil Government." When his college class held its tenth reunion in 1847, and each man was asked to send to the secretary a record of achievement, Thoreau wrote: "My steadiest employment, if such it can be called, is to keep myself at the top of my condition and ready for whatever may turn up in heaven or on earth." There is the motto of Transcendentalism, stamped upon a single coin.

For "to be ready for whatever may turn up" is Thoreau's racier, homelier version of Emerson's "endless seeker"; and Thoreau, more easily than Emerson, could venture to stake everything upon the quest. The elder man had announced the programme, but by 1847 he was himself almost

what Thoreau would call a "committed man,"
with family and household responsibilities, with
a living to earn, and bound, like every professional
writer and speaker, to have some measure of
regard for his public. But Thoreau was ready to
travel lightly and alone. If he should fail in the
great adventure for spiritual perfection, it was his
own affair. He had no intimates, no confidant
save the multitudinous pages of his *Journal*, from
which — and here again he followed Emerson's
example — his future books were to be compiled.
Many of his most loyal admirers will admit that
such a quest is bound, by the very conditions of the
problem, to be futile. Hawthorne allegorized it
in *Ethan Brand*, and his quaint illustration of the
folly of romantic expansion of the self apart from
the common interests of human kind is the picture of a dog chasing its own tail. "It is time now
that I begin to live," notes Thoreau in the *Journal*,
and he continued to say it in a hundred different
ways until the end of all his journalizing, but he
never quite captured the fugitive felicity. The
haunting pathos of his own allegory has moved
every reader of *Walden*: "I long ago lost a hound, a
bay horse, and a turtle-dove, and am still on their
trail." Precisely what he meant it is now impos-

Darwin, Anderson-Lamb Co. N.Y.

sible to say, but surely he betrays a doubt in the ultimate efficacy of his own system of life. He bends doggedly to the trail, for Henry Thoreau is no quitter, but the trail leads nowhere, and in the latest volumes of the *Journals* he seems to realize that he has been pursuing a phantom. He dived fearlessly and deep into himself, but somehow he failed to grasp that pearl of great price which all the transcendental prophets assured him was to be had at the cost of diving.

This is not to say that this austere and strenuous athlete came up quite empty-handed. Far from it. The by-products of his toil were enough to have enriched many lesser men, and they have given Thoreau a secure fame. From his boyhood he longed to make himself a writer, and an admirable writer he became. "For a long time," he says in *Walden*, "I was reporter to a journal, of no very wide circulation, whose editor has never seen fit to print the bulk of my contributions, and, as is too common with writers, I got only my labor for my pains. However, in this case my pains were their reward." Like so many solitaries, he experienced the joy of intense, long-continued effort in composition, and he was artist enough to know that his pages, carefully assembled from his notebooks, had pungency, form, atmosphere. No man of his day, not even Lowell the "last of the bookmen," abandoned himself more unreservedly to the delight of reading. Thoreau was an accomplished scholar in the Greek and Roman classics, as his translations attest. He had some acquaintance with several modern languages, and at one time possessed the best collection of books on Oriental literature to be found in America. He was drenched in the English poetry of the seventeenth century. His critical essays in the *Dial,* his letters and the bookish allusions throughout his writings, are evidence of rich harvesting in the records of the past. He left some three thousand manuscript pages of notes on the American Indians, whose history and character had fascinated him from boyhood. Even his antiquarian hobbies gave him durable satisfaction. Then, too, he had deep delight in his life-long studies in natural history, in his meticulous measurements of river currents, in his notes upon the annual flowering of plants and the migration of birds. The more thoroughly trained naturalists of our own day detect him now and again in error as to his birds and plants, just as specialists in Maine woodcraft discover that he made amusing, and for him un-

accountable, blunders when he climbed Katahdin.
But if he was not impeccable as a naturalist or
woodsman, who has ever had more fun out of his
enthusiasm than Thoreau, and who has ever stimulated as many men and women in the happy use of
their eyes? He would have had slight patience
with much of the sentimental nature study of our
generation, and certainly an intellectual contempt
for much that we read and write about the call of
the wild; but no reader of his books can escape his
infection for the freedom of the woods, for the
stark and elemental in nature. Thoreau's passion
for this aspect of life may have been selfish, wolf-
like, but it is still communicative.

Once, toward the close of his too brief life,
Thoreau "signed on" again to an American ideal,
and no man could have signed more nobly. It was
the cause of Freedom, as represented by John
Brown of Harper's Ferry. The French and Scotch
blood in the furtive hermit suddenly grew hot.
Instead of renouncing in disgust the "uncivil
chaos called Civil Government," Thoreau chal-
lenged it to a fight. Indeed he had already thrown
down the gauntlet in *Slavery in Massachusetts*,
which Garrison had published in the *Liberator* in
1854. And now the death upon the scaffold of the

old fanatic of Ossawatomie changed Thoreau into a complete citizen, arguing the case and glorifying to his neighbors the dead hero. "It seems as if no man had ever died in America before; for in order to die you must first have lived. . . . I hear a good many pretend that they are going to die. . . . Nonsense! I'll defy them to do it. They haven't got life enough in them. They'll deliquesce like fungi, and keep a hundred eulogists mopping the spot where they left off. Only half a dozen or so have died since the world began." Such passages as this reveal a very different Thoreau from the Thoreau who is supposed to have spent his days in the company of swamp-black-birds and woodchucks. He had, in fact, one of the highest qualifications for human society, an absolute honesty of mind. "We select granite," he says, "for the underpinning of our houses and barns; we build fences of stone; but we do not ourselves rest on an underpinning of granite truth, the lowest primitive rock. Our sills are rotten. . . . In proportion as our inward life fails, we go more constantly and desperately to the post-office. You may depend upon it, that the poor fellow who walks away with the greatest number of letters, proud of his extensive correspondence, has not heard from himself this long time."

This hard, basic individualism was for Thoreau the foundation of all enduring social relations, and the dullest observer of twentieth century America can see that Thoreau's doctrine is needed as much as ever. His sharp-edged personality provokes curiosity and pricks the reader into dissent or emulation as the case may be, but its chief ethical value to our generation lies in the fact that here was a Transcendentalist who stressed, not the life of the senses, though he was well aware of their seductiveness, but the stubborn energy of the will.

The scope of the present book prevents more than a glimpse at the other members of the New England Transcendental group. They are a very mixed company, noble, whimsical, queer, impossible. "The good Alcott," wrote Carlyle, "with his long, lean face and figure, with his gray worn temples and mild radiant eyes; all bent on saving the world by a return to acorns and the golden age; he comes before one like a venerable Don Quixote, whom nobody can laugh at without loving." These words paint a whole company, as well as a single man. The good Alcott still awaits an adequate biographer. Connecticut Yankee, peddler

in the South, school-teacher in Boston and elsewhere, he descended upon Concord, flitted to the
queer community of Fruitlands, was starved back
to Concord, inspired and bored the patient Emerson, talked endlessly, wrote ineffective books, and
had at last his apotheosis in the Concord School of
Philosophy, but was chiefly known for the twenty
years before his death in 1888 as the father of
the Louisa Alcott who wrote *Little Women*. "A
tedious archangel," was Emerson's verdict, and
it is likely to stand.

Margaret Fuller, though sketched by Hawthorne,
analyzed by Emerson, and painted at full length
by Thomas Wentworth Higginson, is now a fading
figure — a remarkable woman, no doubt, one of the
first of American feminists, suggesting George
Eliot in her physical unattractiveness, her clear
brain, her touch of sensuousness. She was an
early-ripe, over-crammed scholar in the classics
and in modern European languages. She did
loyal, unpaid work as the editor of the *Dial*, which
from 1840 to 1844 was the organ of Transcendentalism. She joined the community at Brook Farm,
whose story has been so well told by Lindsay
Swift. For a while she served as literary editor
of the *New York Tribune* under Horace Greeley.

Then she went abroad, touched Rousseau's manuscripts at Paris with trembling, adoring fingers, made a secret marriage in Italy with the young Marquis Ossoli, and perished by shipwreck, with her husband and child, off Fire Island in 1850.

Theodore Parker, like Alcott and "Margaret," an admirable Greek scholar, an idealist and reformer, still lives in Chadwick's biography, in Colonel Higginson's delightful essay, and in the memories of a few liberal Bostonians who remember his tremendous sermons on the platform of the old Music Hall. He was a Lexington farmer's son, with the temperament of a blacksmith, with enormous, restless energy, a good hater, a passionate lover of all excellent things save meekness. He died at fifty, worn out, in Italy.

But while these three figures were, after Emerson and Thoreau, the most representative of the group, the student of the Transcendental period will be equally interested in watching its influence upon many other types of young men: upon future journalists and publicists like George William Curtis, Charles A. Dana, and George Ripley; upon religionists like Orestes Brownson, Father Hecker, and James Freeman Clarke; and upon poets like Jones Very, Christopher P. Cranch, and

Ellery Channing. There was a sunny side of the whole movement, as T. W. Higginson and F. B. Sanborn, two of the latest survivors of the ferment, loved to emphasize in their talk and in their books; and it was shadowed also by tragedy and the pathos of unfulfilled desires. But as one looks back at it, in the perspective of three-quarters of a century, it seems chiefly something touchingly fine. For all these men and women tried to hitch their wagon to a star.

CHAPTER VII

MOVING in and out of the Transcendentalist circles, in that great generation preceding the Civil War, were a company of other men — romancers, poets, essayists, historians — who shared in the intellectual liberalism of the age, but who were more purely artists in prose and verse than they were seekers after the unattainable. Hawthorne, for example, sojourned at Concord and at Brook Farm with some of the most extreme types of transcendental extravagance. The movement interested him artistically and he utilized it in his romances, but personally he maintained an attitude of cool detachment from it. Longfellow was too much of an artist to lose his head over philosophical abstractions; Whittier, at his best, had a too genuine poetic instinct for the concrete; and Lowell and Holmes had the saving gift of humor. Cultivated Boston gentlemen like Prescott, Motley, and

143

Parkman preferred to keep their feet on the solid earth and write admirable histories. So the mellow years went by. Most of the widely-read American books were being produced within twenty miles of the Boston State House. The slavery issue kept growling, far away, but it was only now and then, as in the enforcement of the Fugitive Slave Act of 1850, that it was brought sharply home to the North. The "golden forties" were as truly golden for New England as for idle California. There was wealth, leisure, books, a glow of harvest-time in the air, though the spirit of the writers is the spirit of youth.

Nathaniel Hawthorne, our greatest writer of pure romance, was Puritan by inheritance and temperament, though not in doctrine or in sympathy. His literary affiliations were with the English and German Romanticists, and he possessed, for professional use, the ideas and vocabulary of his transcendental friends. Born in Salem in 1804, he was descended from Judge Hawthorne of Salem Witchcraft fame, and from a long line of sea-faring ancestors. He inherited a morbid solitariness, redeemed in some measure by a physical endowment of rare strength and beauty. He read Spenser, Rousseau, and the *Newgate Cal-*

endar, was graduated at Bowdoin, with Long-fellow, in the class of 1825, and returned to Salem for thirteen brooding lonely years in which he tried to teach himself the art of story-writing.   His earliest tales, like Irving's, are essays in which characters emerge; he is absorbed in finding a setting for a preconceived "moral"; he is in love with allegory and parable.   His own words about his first collection of stories, *Twice-Told Tales*, have often been quoted: "They have the pale tint of flowers that blossomed in too retired a shade." Yet they are for the most part exquisitely written. After a couple of years in the Boston Custom-House, and a residence at the socialistic community of Brook Farm, Hawthorne made the happiest of marriages to Sophia Peabody, and for nearly four years dwelt in the Old Manse at Concord.   He described it in one of the ripest of his essays, the Preface to *Mosses from an Old Manse*, his second collection of stories.   After three years in the Custom-House at Salem, his dismissal in 1849 gave him leisure to produce his masterpiece, *The Scarlet Letter*, published in 1850.   He was now forty-six.   In 1851, he published *The House of the Seven Gables*, *The Wonder-Book*, and *The Snow-Image, and Other Tales*.   In 1852 came *The*

Blithedale Romance, a rich ironical story drawn from his Brook Farm experience. Four years in the American Consulate at Liverpool and three subsequent years of residence upon the Continent saw no literary harvest except carefully filled notebooks and the deeply imaginative moral romance, *The Marble Faun*. Hawthorne returned home in 1860 and settled in the Wayside at Concord, busying himself with a new, and, as was destined, a never completed story about the elixir of immortality. But his vitality was ebbing, and in May, 1864, he passed away in his sleep. He rests under the pines in Sleepy Hollow, near the Alcotts and the Emersons.

It is difficult for contemporary Americans to assess the value of such a man, who evidently did nothing except to write a few books. His rare, delicate genius was scarcely touched by passing events. Not many of his countrymen really love his writings, as they love, for instance the writings of Dickens or Thackeray or Stevenson. Everyone reads, at some time of his life, *The Scarlet Letter*, and trembles at its passionate indictment of the sin of concealment, at its agonized admonition, "Be true! Be true!" Perhaps the happiest memories of Hawthorne's readers, as of Kipling's readers, hover about his charming stories for children; to have missed *The Wonder-Book* is like having grown old without ever catching the sweetness of the green world at dawn. But our public has learned to enjoy a wholly different kind of style, taught by the daily journals, a nervous, graphic, sensational, physical style, fit for describing an automobile, a department store, a steamship, a lynching party. It is the style of our day, and judged by it Hawthorne, who wrote with severity, conscience, and good taste, seems somewhat old-fashioned, like Irving or Addison. He is perhaps too completely a New Englander to be understood by men of other stock, and has never, like Poe and Whitman, excited strong interest among European minds.

Yet no American is surer, generation after generation, of finding a fit audience. Hawthorne's genius was meditative rather than dramatic. His artistic material was moral rather than physical; he brooded over the soul of man as affected by this and that condition and situation. The child of a new analytical age, he thought out with rigid accuracy the precise circumstances surrounding each one of his cases and modifying it. Many of his sketches and short stories and most of his romances deal with historical facts, moods, and atmospheres, and he knew the past of New England as few men have ever known it. There is solid historical and psychological stuff as the foundation of his air-castles. His latent radicalism furnished him with a touchstone of criticism as he interpreted the moral standards of ancient communities; no reader of *The Scarlet Letter* can forget Hawthorne's implicit condemnation of the unimaginative harshness of the Puritans. His own judgment upon the deep matters of the human conscience was stern enough, but it was a universalized judgment, and by no means the result of a Calvinism which he hated. Over-fond as he was in his earlier tales of elaborate, fanciful, decorative treatment of themes that promised to point a moral, in his finest short stories, such as *The Ambitious Guest*, *The Gentle Boy*, *Young Goodman Brown*, *The Snow Image*, *The Great Stone Face*, *Drowne's Wooden Image*, *Rappacini's Daughter*, the moral, if there be one, is not obtruded. He loves physical symbols for mental and moral states, and was poet and Transcendentalist enough to retain his youthful affection for parables; but his true field as a story-teller is the erring, questing, aspiring, shadowed human heart.

The Scarlet Letter, for instance, is a study of a universal theme, the problem of concealed sin, punishment, redemption. Only the setting is provincial. The story cannot be rightly estimated, it is true, without remembering the Puritan reverence for physical purity, the Puritan reverence for the magistrate-minister — differing so widely from the respect of Latin countries for the priest — the Puritan preoccupation with the life of the soul, or, as more narrowly construed by Calvinism, the problem of evil. The word Adultery, although suggestively enough present in one of the finest symbolical titles ever devised by a romancer, does not once occur in the book. The sins dealt with are hypocrisy and revenge. Arthur Dimmesdale, Hester Prynne, and Roger Chillingworth are developing, suffering, living creatures, caught inextricably in the toils of a moral situation. By an incomparable succession of pictures Hawthorne exhibits the travail of their souls. In the greatest scene of all, that between Hester and Arthur in the forest, the Puritan framework of the story gives way beneath the weight of human passion, and we seem on the verge of another and perhaps larger solution than was actually worked out by the logic of succeeding events. But though the book has been called Christless, prayerless, hopeless, no mature person ever reads it without a deepened sense of the impotence of all mechanistic theories of sin, and a new vision of the intense reality of spiritual things. "The law we broke," in Dimmesdale's ghostly words, was a more subtle law than can be graven on tables of stone and numbered as the Seventh Commandment.

The legacy of guilt is likewise the theme of *The House of the Seven Gables*, which Hawthorne himself was inclined to think a better book than *The Scarlet Letter*. Certainly this story of old Salem is impeccably written and its subtle handling of tone and atmosphere is beyond dispute. An ancestral curse, the visitation of the sins of the fathers upon the children, the gradual decay of a once sound stock, are motives that Ibsen might have developed. But the Norseman would have failed to rival Hawthorne's delicate manipulation of his shadows, and the no less masterly deftness of the ultimate mediation of a dark inheritance through the love of the light-hearted Phœbe for the latest descendant of the Maules. In *The Blithedale Romance* Hawthorne stood for once, perhaps, too near his material to allow the rich atmospheric effects which he prefers, and in spite of the unfor-

NATHANIEL HAWTHORNE, 1860

Photograph from a negative taken by Mayall in London, England.
In the possession of Mr. Frank Cousins, Salem, Mass.

NATHANIEL HAWTHORNE, 1840

Painting by Charles Osgood. In the possession of Mrs. R. C. Manning, Salem, Mass.

getable portrait of Zenobia and powerful passages of realistic description, the book is not quite focussed. In *The Marble Faun* Hawthorne comes into his own again. Its central problem is one of those dark insoluble ones that he loves: the influence of a crime upon the development of a soul. Donatello, the Faun, is a charming young creature of the natural sunshine until his love for the somber Miriam tempts him to the commission of murder: then begins the growth of his mind and character. Perhaps the haunting power of the main theme of the book has contributed less to its fame than the felicity of its descriptions of Rome and Italy. For Hawthorne possessed, like Byron, in spite of his defective training in the appreciation of the arts, a gift of romantic discernment which makes *The Marble Faun*, like *Childe Harold*, a glorified guide-book to the Eternal City.

All of Hawthorne's books, in short, have a central core of psychological romance, and a rich surface finish of description. His style, at its best, has a subdued splendor of coloring which is only less wonderful than the spiritual perceptions with which this magician was endowed. The gloom which haunts many of his pages, as I have said elsewhere, is the long shadow cast by our mortal destiny upon a sensitive soul. The mystery is our mystery, perceived, and not created, by that finely endowed mind and heart. The shadow is our shadow; the gleams of insight, the soft radiance of truth and beauty, are his own.

A college classmate of Henry Wadsworth Longfellow summed up the Portland boy's character in one sentence: "It appeared easy for him to avoid the unworthy." Born in 1807, of *Mayflower* stock that had distinguished itself for bravery and uprightness, the youth was graduated from Bowdoin at eighteen. Like his classmate Hawthorne, he had been a wide and secretly ambitious reader, and had followed the successive numbers of Irving's *Sketch Book*, he tells us, "with ever increasing wonder and delight." His college offered him in 1826 a professorship of the modern languages, and he spent three happy years in Europe in preparation. He taught successfully at Bowdoin for five or six years, and for eighteen years, 1836 to 1854, served as George Ticknor's successor at Harvard, ultimately surrendering the chair to Lowell. He early published two prose volumes, *Hyperion* and *Outre-mer*, Irvingesque romances of European travel. Then came, after ten years of teaching and the death of his young wife, the sudden impulse to write poetry, and he produced, "softly excited, I know not why," *The Reaper and the Flowers, a Psalm of Death*. From that December morning in 1838 until his death in 1882 he was Longfellow the Poet.

His outward life, like Hawthorne's, was barren of dramatic incident, save the one tragic accident by which his second wife, the mother of his children, perished before his eyes in 1861. He bore the calamity with the quiet courage of his race and breeding. But otherwise his days ran softly and gently, enriched with books and friendships, sheltered from the storms of circumstance. He had leisure to grow ripe, to remember, and to dream. But he never secluded himself, like Tennyson, from normal contacts with his fellowmen. The owner of the Craigie House was a good neighbor, approachable and deferential. He was even interested in local Cambridge politics. On the larger political issues of his day his Americanism was sound and loyal. "It is disheartening," he wrote in his Cambridge journal for 1851, "to see how little sympathy there is in the hearts of the young men here for freedom and great ideas." But his own sympathy never wavered.

His linguistic talent helped him to penetrate the secrets of alien ways of thought and speech. He understood Italy and Spain, Holland and France and Germany. He had studied them on the lips of their living men and women and in the books where soldier and historian, priest and poet, had inscribed the record of five hundred years. From the Revival of Learning to the middle of the nineteenth century, Longfellow knew the soul of Europe as few men have known it, and he helped to translate Europe to America. His intellectual receptivity, his quick eye for color and costume and landscape, his ear for folk-lore and ballad, his own ripe mastery of words, made him the most resourceful of international interpreters. And this lover of children, walking in quiet ways, this refined and courteous host and gentleman, scholar and poet, exemplified without self-advertisement the richer qualities of his own people. When Couper's statue of Longfellow was dedicated in Washington, Hamilton Mabie said: "His freedom from the sophistication of a more experienced country; his simplicity, due in large measure to the absence of social self-consciousness; his tranquil and deep-seated optimism, which is the effluence of an unexhausted soil; his happy and confident expectation, born of a sense of tremendous national vitality; his love of simple things in normal relations to world-wide interests of the mind; his courage in interpreting those deeper experiences which craftsmen who know art but who do not know life call commonplaces; the unaffected and beautiful democracy of his spirit—these are the delicate flowers of our new world, and as much a part of it as its stretches of wilderness and the continental roll of its rivers."

Longfellow's poetic service to his countrymen has thus become a national asset, and not merely because in his three best known narrative poems, *Evangeline*, *Hiawatha*, and *The Courtship of Miles Standish*, he selected his themes from our own history. *The Building of the Ship*, written with full faith in the troubled year of 1849, is a national anthem. "It is a wonderful gift," said Lincoln, as he listened to it, his eyes filled with tears, "to be able to stir men like that." *The Skeleton in Armor*, *A Ballad of the French Fleet*, *Paul Revere's Ride*, *The Wreck of the Hesperus*, are ballads that stir men still. For all of his skill in story-telling in verse—witness the *Tales of a Wayside Inn*—Longfellow was not by nature a dramatist, and his trilogy now published under the title of *Christus*, made up of *The Divine Tragedy*, *The Golden Legend*, and *New England Tragedies*, added little to a reputation won in other fields. His sonnets, particularly those upon *Chaucer*, *Milton*, *The Divina Commedia*, *A Nameless Grave*, *Felton*, *Sumner*, *Nature*, *My Books*, are among the imperishable treasures of the English language. In descriptive pieces like *Keramos* and *The Hanging of the Crane*, in such personal and occasional verses as *The Herons of Elmwood*, *The Fiftieth Birthday of Agassiz*, and the noble *Morituri Salutamus* written for his classmates in 1875, he exhibits his tenderness of affection and all the ripeness of his technical skill. But it was as a lyric poet, after all, that he won and held his immense audience throughout the English-speaking world. Two of the most popular of all his early pieces, *The Psalm of Life* and *Excelsior*, have paid the price of a too apt adjustment to the ethical mood of an earnest moment in our national life. We have passed beyond them. And many readers may have outgrown their youthful pleasure in *Maidenhood*, *The Rainy Day*, *The Bridge*, *The Day is Done*, verses whose simplicity lent themselves temptingly to parody. Yet such poems as *The Belfry of Bruges*, *Seaweed*, *The Fire of Driftwood*, *The Arsenal at Springfield*, *My Lost Youth*,

The Children's Hour, and many another lyric, lose nothing with the lapse of time. There is fortunately infinite room for personal preference in this whole matter of poetry, but the confession of a lack of regard for Longfellow's verse must often be recognized as a confession of a lessening love for what is simple, graceful, and refined. The current of contemporary American taste, especially among consciously clever, half-trained persons, seems to be running against Longfellow. How soon the tide may turn, no one can say. Meanwhile he has his tranquil place in the Poet's Corner of Westminster Abbey. The Abbey must be a pleasant spot to wait in, for the Portland boy.

Oddly enough, some of the over-sophisticated and under-experienced people who affect to patronize Longfellow assume toward John Greenleaf Whittier an air of deference. This attitude would amuse the Quaker poet. One can almost see his dark eyes twinkle and the grim lips tighten in that silent laughter in which the old man so much resembled Cooper's Leather-Stocking. Whittier knew that his friend Longfellow was a better artist than himself, and he also knew, by intimate experience as a maker of public opinion, how variable are its judgments.

Whittier represents a stock different from that of the Longfellows, but equally American, equally thoroughbred: the Essex County Quaker farmer of Massachusetts. The homestead in which he was born in 1807, at East Haverhill, had been built by his great-great-grandfather in 1688. Mount Vernon in Virginia and the Craigie House in Cambridge are newer than this by two generations. The house has been restored to the precise aspect it had in Whittier's boyhood: and the garden, lawn, and brook, even the door-stone and bridle-post and the barn across the road are witnesses to the fidelity of the descriptions in *Snow-Bound*. The neighborhood is still a lonely one. The youth grew up in seclusion, yet in contact with a few great ideas, chief among them Liberty. "My father," he said, "was an old-fashioned Democrat, and really believed in the Preamble of the Bill of Rights which reaffirmed the Declaration of Independence." The taciturn father transmitted to his sons a hatred of kingcraft and priestcraft, the inward moral freedom of the Quaker touched with humanitarian passion. The spirit of a boyhood in this homestead is veraciously told in *The Barefoot Boy*, *School-Days*, *Snow-Bound*, *Ramoth Hill*, and *Telling the Bees*. It was a chance copy of Burns that revealed to the farmer lad his own desire and capacity for verse-writing. When he was nineteen, his sister sent his *Exile's Departure* to William Lloyd Garrison, then twenty, and the editor of the *Newburyport Free Press*. The neighbors liked it, and the tall frail author was rewarded with a term at the Haverhill Academy, where he paid his way, in old Essex County fashion, by making shoes.

He had little more formal schooling than this, was too poor to enter college, but had what he modestly called a "knack at rhyming," and much facility in prose. He turned to journalism and politics, for which he possessed a notable instinct. For a while he thought he had "done with poetry and literature." Then in 1833, at twenty-six, came Garrison's stirring letter bidding him enlist in the cause of Anti-Slavery. He obeyed the call, not knowing that this new allegiance to the service of humanity was to transform him from a facile local verse-writer into a national poet. It was the ancient miracle of losing one's life and finding it. For the immediate sacrifice was very real to a youth trained in quietism and non-resistance, and well aware, as a Whig journalist, of the ostracism visited upon the active

Abolitionists. Whittier entered the fight with absolute courage and with the shrewdest practical judgment of weapons and tactics. He forgot himself. He turned aside from those pleasant fields of New England legend and history to which he was destined to return after his warfare was accomplished. He had read the prose of Milton and of Burke. He perceived that negro emancipation in the United States was only a single and immediate phase of a universal movement of liberalism. The thought kindled his imagination. He wrote, at white heat, political and social verse that glowed with humanitarian passion: lyrics in praise of fellow-workers, salutes to the dead, campaign songs, hymns, satires against the clergy and the capitalists, superb sectional poems like *Massachusetts to Virginia*, and, more nobly still, poems embodying what Wordsworth called "the sensation and image of country and the human race."

Whittier had now "found himself" as a poet. It is true that his style remained diffuse and his ear faulty, but his countrymen, then as now uncritical of artistic form, overlooked the blemishes of his verse, and thought only of his vibrant emotion, his scorn of cowardice and evil, his prophetic exaltation. In 1847 came the first general collection of his poems, and here were to be found not merely controversial verses, but spirited *Songs of Labor*, pictures of the lovely Merrimac countryside, legends written in the mood of Hawthorne or Longfellow, and bright bits of foreign lore and fancy. For though Whittier never went abroad, his quiet life at Amesbury gave him leisure for varied reading, and he followed contemporary European politics with the closest interest. He emerged more and more from the atmosphere of faction and section, and, though he retained to the last his Quaker creed, he held its simple tenets in such undogmatic and winning fashion that his hymns are sung today in all the churches.

When *The Atlantic Monthly* was established in 1857, Whittier was fifty. He took his place among the contributors to the new magazine not as a controversialist but as a man of letters, with such poems as *Tritemius*, and *Skipper Ireson's Ride*. Characteristic productions of this period are *My Psalm, Cobbler Keezar's Vision, Andrew Rykman's Prayer, The Eternal Goodness* — poems grave, sweet, and tender. But it was not until the publication of *Snow-Bound* in 1866 that Whittier's work touched its widest popularity. He had never married, and the deaths of his mother and sister Elizabeth set him brooding, in the desolate Amesbury house, over memories of his birthplace, six miles away in East Haverhill. The homestead had gone out of the hands of the Whittiers, and the poet, nearing sixty, set himself to compose an idyll descriptive of the vanished past. No artist could have a theme more perfectly adapted to his mood and to his powers. There are no novel ideas in *Snow-Bound*, nor is there any need of them, but the thousands of annual pilgrims to the old farmhouse can bear witness to the touching intimacy, the homely charm, the unerring rightness of feeling with which Whittier's genius recreated his own lost youth and painted for all time a true New England hearthside.

Whittier was still to write nearly two hundred more poems, for he lived to be eighty-five, and he composed until the last. But his creative period was now over. He rejoiced in the friendly recognition of his work that came to him from every section of a reunited country. His personal friends were loyal in their devotion. He followed the intricacies of American politics with the keen

zest of a veteran in that game, for in his time
he had made and unmade governors and senators.
"The greatest politician I have ever met," said
James G. Blaine, who had certainly met many.
He had an income from his poems far in excess
of his needs, but retained the absolute simplicity
of his earlier habits. When his publishers first
proposed the notable public dinner in honor of
his seventieth birthday he demurred, explaining
to a member of his family that he did not want the
bother of "buying a new pair of pants"—a petty
anecdote, but somehow refreshing. So the rustic,
shrewd, gentle old man waited for the end. He
had known what it means to toil, to fight, to
renounce, to eat his bread in tears, and to see
some of his dreams come true. We have had,
and shall have, more accomplished craftsmen in
verse, but we have never bred a more genuine
man than Whittier, nor one who had more kinship
with the saints.

A few days before Whittier's death, he wrote
an affectionate poem in celebration of the eighty-
third birthday of his old friend of the Saturday
Club, Dr. Oliver Wendell Holmes. This was in
1892. The little Doctor, rather lonely in his latest
years, composed some tender obituary verses

at Whittier's passing. He had already performed the same office for Lowell. He lingered himself until the autumn of 1894, in his eighty-sixth year—*The Last Leaf*, in truth, of New England's richest springtime.

"No, my friends," he had said in *The Autocrat of the Breakfast Table*, "I go (always, other things being equal) for the man who inherits family traditions and the cumulative humanities of at least four or five generations." The Doctor came naturally by his preference for a "man of family," being one himself. He was a descendant of Anne Bradstreet, the poetess. "Dorothy Q.," whom he had made the most picturesque of the Quincys, was his great-grandmother. Wendell Phillips was his cousin. His father, the Rev. Abiel Holmes, a Yale graduate, was the minister of the First Church in Cambridge, and it was in its "gambrel-roofed" parsonage that Oliver Wendell was born in 1809.

> Know old Cambridge? Hope you do.—
> Born there? Don't say so! I was, too.
>
> .   .   .   .   .   .
>
> Nicest place that was ever seen—
> Colleges red and Common green.

So he wrote, in scores of passages of filial devotion, concerning the village of his boyhood and the city of Boston. His best-known prose sentence is: "Boston State House is the hub of the Solar System." It is easy to smile, as indeed he did himself, at such fond provinciality, but the fact remains that our literature as a whole sadly needs this richness of local atmosphere. A nation of restless immigrants, here today and "moved on" tomorrow, has the fibres of its imagination uprooted, and its artists in their eager quest of "local color" purchase brilliancy at the cost of thinness of tone, poverty of association. Philadelphia and Boston, almost alone among the larger American cities, yield the sense of intimacy, or what the Autocrat would call "the cumulative humanities."

Young Holmes became the pet and the glory of his class of 1829 at Harvard. It was only in 1838 that their reunions began, but thereafter they held fifty-six meetings, of which Holmes attended fifty and wrote poems for forty-three. Many of "the Boys" whom he celebrated became famous in their own right, but they remain "the Boys" to all lovers of Holmes's verses. His own career as a poet had begun during his single year in the Law School. His later years brought him some additional skill in polishing his lines and a riper human wisdom, but his native verse-making talent is as completely revealed in *Old Ironsides*, published when he was twenty-one, and in *The Last Leaf*, composed a year or two later, as in anything he was to write during the next half-century. In many respects he was a curious survival of the cumulative humanities of the eighteenth century. He might have been, like good Dr. Arbuthnot, an ornament of the Augustan age. He shared with the English Augustans a liking for the rhymed couplet, an instinctive social sense, a feeling for the presence of an imaginary audience of congenial listeners. One still catches the "Hear! Hear!" between his clever lines. In many of the traits of his mind this "Yankee Frenchman" resembled such a typical eighteenth century figure as Voltaire. Like Voltaire, he was tolerant—except toward Calvinism and Homeopathy. In some of the tricks of his prose style he is like a kindlier Sterne. His knack for *vers de société* was caught from Horace, but he would not have been a child of his own age without the additional gift of rhetoric and eloquence which is to be seen in his patriotic poems and his hymns. For Holmes possessed, in spite of all his limitations in poetic range, true devotion, patriotism, humor, and pathos.

JOHN GREENLEAF WHITTIER   JAMES RUSSELL LOWELL

Wood engraving from a photograph.   Photograph.

HENRY WADSWORTH LONGFELLOW   OLIVER WENDELL HOLMES

Photograph.   Wood engraving from a photograph.

JOHN GREENLEAF WHITTIER

Wood engraving from a photograph.

JAMES RUSSELL LOWELL

Photograph.

HENRY WADSWORTH LONGFELLOW

Photograph.

OLIVER WENDELL HOLMES

Wood engraving from a photograph.

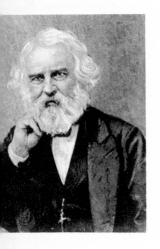

His poetry was in the best sense of the word "occasional," and his prose was only an incidental or accidental harvest of a long career in which his chief duty was that of a professor of anatomy in the Harvard Medical School. He had studied in Paris under sound teachers, and after some years of private practice won the appointment which he held, as active and emeritus professor, for forty-seven years. He was a faithful, clear, and amusing lecturer, and printed two or three notable medical essays, but his chief Boston reputation, in the eighteen-fifties, was that of a wit and diner-out and writer of verses for occasions. Then came his great hour of good luck in 1857, when Lowell, the editor of the newly-established *Atlantic Monthly*, persuaded him to write *The Autocrat of the Breakfast Table*. It was the public's luck also, for whoever had been so unfortunate as not to be born in Boston could now listen—as if across the table—to Boston's best talker. Few volumes of essays during the last sixty years have given more pleasure to a greater variety of readers than is yielded by *The Autocrat*. It gave the Doctor a reputation in England which he naturally prized, and which contributed to his triumphal English progress, many years later, recorded pleasantly in

Our Hundred Days. *The Professor at the Breakfast Table* and *The Poet at the Breakfast Table* are less successful variations of *The Autocrat.* Neither professors nor poets are at their best at this meal. Holmes wrote three novels — of which *Elsie Venner,* a somewhat too medical story, is the best remembered — memoirs of his friends Emerson and Motley, and many miscellaneous essays. His life was exceptionally happy, and his cheery good opinion of himself is still contagious. To pronounce the words Doctor Holmes in any company of intelligent Americans is the prologue to a smile of recognition, comprehension, sympathy. The word Goldsmith has now lost, alas, this provocative quality; the word Stevenson still possesses it. The little Doctor, who died in the same year as Stevenson, belonged like him to the genial race of friends of mankind, and a few of his poems, and some gay warm-hearted pages of his prose, will long preserve his memory. But the Boston which he loved has vanished as utterly as Sam Johnson's London.

James Russell Lowell was ten years younger than Holmes, and though he died three years before the Doctor, he seems, for other reasons than those of chronology, to belong more nearly to the present. Although by birth as much of a New England Brahmin as Holmes, and in his later years as much of a Boston and Cambridge idol, he nevertheless touched our universal American life on many sides, represented us worthily in foreign diplomacy, argued the case of Democracy with convincing power, and embodied, as more perfect artists like Hawthorne and Longfellow could never have done, the subtleties and potencies of the national temperament. He deserves and reveals the closest scrutiny, but his personality is difficult to put on paper. Horace Scudder wrote his biography with careful competence, and Ferris Greenslet has made him the subject of a brilliant critical study. Yet readers differ widely in their assessment of the value of his prose and verse, and in their understanding of his personality.

The external facts of his career are easy to trace and must be set down here with brevity. A minister's son, and descended from a very old and distinguished family, he was born at Elmwood in Cambridge in 1819. After a somewhat turbulent course, he was graduated from Harvard in 1838, the year of Emerson's *Divinity School Address*. He studied law, turned Abolitionist, wrote poetry, married the beautiful and transcendental Maria White, and did magazine work in Boston, New York, and Philadelphia. He was thought by his friends in the eighteen-fifties to be "the most Shakespearian" man in America. When he was ten years out of college, in 1848, he published *The Biglow Papers* (First Series), *A Fable for Critics*, and *The Vision of Sir Launfal*. After a long visit to Europe and the death of his wife, he gave some brilliant Lowell Institute lectures in Boston, and was appointed Longfellow's successor at Harvard. He went to Europe again to prepare himself, and after entering upon his work as a teacher made a happy second marriage, served for four years as the first editor of *The Atlantic*, and helped his friend Charles Eliot Norton edit *The North American Review*. The Civil War inspired a second series of *Biglow Papers* and the magnificent *Commemoration Ode* of 1865. Then came volume after volume of literary essays, such as *Among My Books* and *My Study Windows*, and an occasional book of verse. Again he made a long sojourn in Europe, resigned his Harvard professorship, and in 1877 was appointed Minister to Spain. After three years he was transferred to the most important post in our diplomatic service, London. He performed his duties with extraordinary skill and success until 1885, when he was relieved. His last years were spent in Elmwood, the Cambridge house where he was born, and he was still writing, in almost as rich a vein as ever, when the end came in 1891.

Here was certainly a full and varied life, responsive to many personal moods and many tides of public feeling. Lowell drew intellectual stimulus from enormously wide reading in classical and modern literatures. Puritanically earnest by inheritance, he seems also to have inherited a strain of levity which he could not always control, and, through his mother's family, a dash of mysticism sometimes resembling second sight. His physical and mental powers were not always in the happiest mutual adjustment: he became easily the prey of moods and fancies, and knew the alternations from wild gaiety of spirits to black despair. The firm moral consistency of Puritanism was always his, yet his playful remark about belonging in a hospital for incurable children had a measure of truth in it also.

Both his poetry and his prose reveal a nature never quite integrated into wholeness of structure, into harmony with itself. His writing, at its best, is noble and delightful, full of human charm, but it is difficult for him to master a certain waywardness and to sustain any note steadily. This temperamental flaw does not affect the winsomeness of his letters, unless to add to it. It is lost to view, often, in the sincerity and pathos of his lyrics, but it is felt in most of his longer efforts in prose, and accounts for a certain dissatisfaction which many grateful and loyal readers neverthe-less feel in his criticism. Lowell was more richly endowed by nature and by breadth of reading than Matthew Arnold, for instance, but in the actual performance of the critical function he was surpassed in method by Arnold and perhaps in inerrant perception, in a limited field, by Poe.

It was as a poet, however, that he first won his place in our literature, and it is by means of certain passages in the *Biglow Papers* and the *Commemoration Ode* that he has most moved his countrymen. The effectiveness of *The Present Crisis* and *Sir Launfal*, and of the *Memorial Odes*, particularly the *Ode to Agassiz*, is likewise due to the passion, sweetness, and splendor of certain strophes, rather than to the perfection of these poems as artistic wholes. Lowell's personal lyrics of sorrow, such as *The Changeling, The First Snow-Fall, After the Burial*, have touched many hearts.

His later lyrics are more subtle, weighted with thought, tinged with autumnal melancholy. He was a most fertile composer, and, like all the men of his time and group, produced too much. Yet his patriotic verse was so admirable in feeling and is still so inspiring to his readers that one cannot wish it less in quantity; and in the field of political satire, such as the two series of *Biglow Papers*, he had a theme and a method precisely suited to his temperament. No American has approached Lowell's success in this difficult *genre:* the swift transitions from rural Yankee humor to splendid scorn of evil and to noblest idealism reveal the full powers of one of our most gifted men. The preacher lurked in this Puritan from first to last, and the war against Mexico and the Civil War stirred him to the depths.

His prose, likewise, is a school of loyalty. There was much of Europe in his learning, as his memorable Dante essay shows, and the traditions of great English literature were the daily companions of his mind. He was bookish, as a bookman should be, and sometimes the very richness and whimsicality of his bookish fancies marred the simplicity and good taste of his pages. But the fundamental texture of his thought and feeling was American, and his most characteristic style has the raciness of our soil. Nature lovers like to point out the freshness and delicacy of his reaction to the New England scene. Thoreau himself, whom Lowell did not like, was not more veracious an observer than the author of *Sunthin' in the Pastoral Line*, *Cambridge Thirty Years Ago*, and *My Garden Acquaintance*. Yet he watched men as keenly as he did "laylocks" and bobolinks, and no shrewder American essay has been written than his *On a Certain Condescension in Foreigners*. Wit and humor and wisdom made him one of the best talkers of his generation. These qualities pervade his essays and his letters, and the latter in particular reveal those ardors and fidelities of friendship which men like Emerson and Thoreau longed after without ever quite experiencing. Lowell's cosmopolitan reputation, which was greatly enhanced in the last decade of his life, seemed to his old associates of the Saturday Club only a fit recognition of the learning, wit, and fine imagination which had been familiar to them from the first. To hold the old friends throughout his lifetime, and to win fresh ones of a new generation through his books, is perhaps the greatest of Lowell's personal felicities.

While there are no other names in the literature
of New England quite comparable with those that
have just been discussed, it should be remembered
that the immediate effectiveness and popularity of
these representative poets and prose writers were
dependent upon the existence of an intelligent
and responsive reading public. The lectures of
Emerson, the speeches of Webster, the stories
of Hawthorne, the political verse of Whittier
and Lowell, presupposed a keen, reflecting audience, mentally and morally exigent. The spread
of the Lyceum system along the line of west-
ward emigration from New England as far as
the Mississippi is one tangible evidence of the
high level of popular intelligence. That there was
much of the superficial and the spread-eagle in the
American life of the eighteen-forties is apparent
enough without the amusing comments of such
English travellers as Dickens, Miss Martineau,
and Captain Basil Hall. But there was also
genuine intellectual curiosity and a general reading
habit which are evidenced not only by a steady
growth of newspapers and magazines but also by
the demand for substantial books. Biography and
history began to be widely read, and it was natural
that the most notable productiveness in historical

writing should manifest itself in that section of the country where there were libraries, wealth, leisure for the pursuits of scholarship, a sense of intimate concern with the great issues of the past, and a diffusion of intellectual tastes throughout the community. It was no accident that Sparks and Ticknor, Bancroft and Prescott, Motley and Parkman, were Massachusetts men.

Jared Sparks, it is true, inherited neither wealth nor leisure. He was a furious, unwearied toiler in the field of our national history. Born in 1789, by profession a Unitarian minister, he began collecting the papers of George Washington by 1825. John Marshall, the great jurist, had published his five-volume life of his fellow Virginian a score of years earlier. But Sparks proceeded to write another biography of Washington and to edit his writings. He also edited a *Library of American Biography*, wrote lives of Franklin and Gouverneur Morris, was professor of history and President of Harvard, and lived to be seventy-seven. As editor of the writings of Franklin and Washington, he took what we now consider unpardonable liberties in altering the text, and this error of judgment has somewhat clouded his just reputation as a pioneer in historical research.

George Bancroft, who was born in 1800, and died, a horseback-riding sage, at ninety-one, inherited from his clergyman father a taste for history. He studied in Germany after leaving Harvard, turned schoolmaster, Democratic politician and office-holder, served as Secretary of the Navy, Minister to England and then to the German Empire, and won distinction in each of his avocations, though the real passion of his life was his *History of the United States*, which he succeeded in bringing down to the adoption of the Constitution. The first volume, which appeared in 1834, reads today like a stump speech by a sturdy Democratic orator of the Jacksonian period. But there was solid stuff in it, nevertheless, and as Bancroft proceeded, decade after decade, he discarded some of his rhetoric and philosophy of democracy and utilized increasingly the vast stores of documents which his energy and his high political positions had made it possible for him to obtain. Late in life he condensed his ten great volumes to six. Posterity will doubtless condense these in turn, as posterity has a way of doing, but Bancroft the historian realized his own youthful ambition with a completeness rare in the history of human effort and performed a monumental service to his country.

12

He was less of an artist, however, than Prescott, the eldest and in some ways the finest figure of the well-known Prescott–Motley–Parkman group of Boston historians. All of these men, together with their friend George Ticknor, who wrote the *History of Spanish Literature* and whose own *Life and Letters* pictures a whole generation, had the professional advantages of inherited wealth, and the opportunity to make deliberate choice of a historical field which offered freshness and picturesqueness of theme. All were tireless workers in spite of every physical handicap; all enjoyed social security and the rich reward of full recognition by their contemporaries. They had their world as in their time, as Chaucer makes the Wife of Bath say of herself, and it was a pleasant world to live in.

Grandson of "Prescott the Brave" of Bunker Hill, and son of the rich Judge Prescott of Salem, William Hickling Prescott was born in 1796, and was graduated from Harvard in 1814. An accident in college destroyed the sight of one eye, and left him but a precarious use of the other. Nevertheless he resolved to emulate Gibbon, whose *Autobiography* had impressed him, and to make himself "an historian in the best sense of the term." He

studied arduously in Europe, with the help of
secretaries, and by 1826, after a long hesitation,
decided upon a *History of the Reign of Ferdinand
and Isabella.* In ten years the three volumes were
finished. "Pursuing the work in this quiet, leisurely way, without over-exertion or fatigue,"
wrote Prescott, "or any sense of obligation to
complete it in a given time, I have found it a
continual source of pleasure." It was published
at his own expense on Christmas Day, 1837, and
met with instantaneous success. "My market
and my reputation rest principally with England,"
he wrote in 1838 — a curious footnote, by the
way, to Emerson's Phi Beta Kappa Address of
the year before. But America joined with England, in praising the new book. Then Prescott
turned to the *Conquest of Mexico,* the *Conquest of
Peru,* and finally to his unfinished *History of the
Reign of Philip II.* He had, as Dean Milman
wrote him, "the judgment to choose noble subjects." He wrote with serenity and dignity, with
fine balance and proportion. Some of the Spanish
documents upon which he relied have been proved
less trustworthy than he thought, but this unsus-
pected defect in his materials scarcely impaired
the skill with which this unhasting, unresting

painter filled his great canvases. They need retouching, perhaps, but the younger historians are incompetent for the task. Prescott died in 1859, in the same year as Irving, and he already seems quite as remote from the present hour.

His young friend Motley, of *Dutch Republic* fame, was another Boston Brahmin, born in the year of Prescott's graduation from college. He attended George Bancroft's school, went to Harvard in due course, where he knew Holmes, Sumner, and Wendell Phillips, and at Göttingen became a warm friend of a dog-lover and duelist named Bismarck. Young Motley wrote a couple of unsuccessful novels, dabbled in diplomacy, politics, and review-writing, and finally, encouraged by Prescott, settled down upon Dutch history, went to Europe to work up his material in 1851, and, after five years, scored an immense triumph with his *Rise of the Dutch Republic*. He was a brilliant partisan, hating Spaniards and Calvinists, and wrote all the better for this bias. He was an admirable sketcher of historical portraits, and had Macaulay's skill in composing special chapters devoted to the tendencies and qualities of an epoch or to the characteristics of a dynasty. Between 1860 and 1868 he produced the four volumes of the *History of the United Nether-lands*. During the Civil War he served usefully as American minister to Vienna, and in 1869 was appointed minister to London. Both of these appointments ended unhappily for him. Dr. Holmes, his loyal admirer and biographer, does not conceal the fact that a steadier, less excitable type of public servant might have handled both the Vienna situation and the London situation without incurring a recall. Motley continued to live in England, where his daughters had married, and where, in spite of his ardent Americanism, he felt socially at home. His last book was *The Life and Death of John of Barneveld*. His *Letters*, edited after his death in 1877 by George William Curtis, give a fascinating picture of English life among the cultivated and leisurely classes. The Boston merchant's son was a high-hearted gentle-man, and his cosmopolitan experiences used to make his stay-at-home friend, Oliver Wendell Holmes, feel rather dull and provincial in com-parison. Both were Sons of Liberty, but Motley had had the luck to find in "brave little Holland" a subject which captivated the interest of Europe and gave the historian international fame. He had more eloquence than the Doctor, and a far more varied range of prose, but there may be here and there a Yankee guesser about the taste of future generations who will bet on *The Autocrat*, after all.

The character and career of Francis Parkman afford curious material to the student of New England's golden age. In the seventy years of his heroic life, from 1823 to 1893, all the characteristic forces of the age reached their culmination and decline, and his own personality indicates some of the violent reactions produced by the over-strain of Transcendentalism. For here was a descendant of John Cotton, and a clergyman's son, who detested Puritanism and the clergy; who, coming to manhood in the eighteen-forties, hated the very words Transcendentalism, Philosophy, Religion, Reform; an inheritor of property, trained at Harvard, and an Overseer and Fellow of his University, who disliked the ideals of culture and refinement; a member of the Saturday Club who was bored with literary talk and literary people; a staunch American who despised democracy as thoroughly as Alexander Hamilton, and thought suffrage a failure; a nineteenth century historian who cared nothing for philosophy, science,

GEORGE BANCROFT

Engraving in Bancroft's *History.*

FRANCIS PARKMAN

Photograph.

WILLIAM H. PRESCOTT

Engraving by Welch.

GEORGE BANCROFT
Engraving in Bancroft's History.

FRANCIS PARKMAN
Photograph.

WILLIAM H. PRESCOTT
Engraving by Welch.

or the larger lessons of history itself; a fascinating realistic writer who admired Scott, Byron, and Cooper for their tales of action, and despised Wordsworth and Thoreau as effeminate sentimentalists who were preoccupied with themselves. In Parkman "the wheel has come full circle," and a movement that began with expansion of self ended in hard Spartan repression, even in inhibition of emotion.

Becoming "enamoured of the woods" at sixteen, Parkman chose his life work at eighteen, and he was a man who could say proudly: "I have not yet abandoned any plan which I ever formed." "Before the end of the sophomore year," he wrote in his autobiography, "my various schemes had crystallized into a plan of writing the story of what was then known as the *Old French War*, that is, the war that ended in the conquest of Canada, for here, as it seemed to me, the forest drama was more stirring and the forest stage more thronged with appropriate actors than in any other passage of our history. It was not till some years later that I enlarged the plan to include the whole course of the American conflict between France and England, or, in other words, the history of the American forest: for this was the light in which I regarded it. My theme fascinated me, and I was haunted with wilderness images day and night." To understand "the history of the American forest" young Parkman devoted his college vacations to long trips in the wilderness, and in 1846, two years after graduation, he made the epoch-making journey described in his first book, *The Oregon Trail*.

The Conspiracy of Pontiac, a highly-colored narrative in two volumes appearing in 1851, marks the first stage of his historical writing. Then came the tragedy of shattered health, and for fourteen years Parkman fought for life and sanity, and produced practically nothing. He had had to struggle from his college days with an obscure disorder of the brain, aggravated by the hardships of his Oregon Trail journey, and by ill-considered efforts to harden his bodily frame by over-exertion. His disease took many forms— insomnia, arthritis, weakness of sight, incapacity for sustained thought. His biographer Farnham says that "he never saw a perfectly well day during his entire literary career." Even when aided by secretaries and copyists, six lines a day was often the limit of his production. His own Stoic words about the limitations of his eyesight are characteristic: "By reading for one minute, and then resting for an equal time, this alternate process may gradually be continued for about half an hour. Then, after a sufficient interval, it may be repeated, often three or four times in the course of the day. By this means nearly the whole of the volume now offered has been composed." There is no more piteous or inspiring story of a fight against odds in the history of literature.

For after his fortieth year the enemy gave way a little, and book after book somehow got itself written. There they stand upon the shelves, a dozen of them—*The Pioneers of France, The Jesuits in North America, La Salle, The Old Régime, Frontenac, Montcalm and Wolfe, A Half-Century of Conflict*—the boy's dream realized, the man's long warfare accomplished. The history of the forest, as Parkman saw it, was a pageant with the dark wilderness for a background, and, for the actors, taciturn savages, black-robed Jesuits, intrepid explorers, soldiers of France—all struggling for a vast prize, all changing, passing, with a pomp and color unknown to wearied Europe. It was a superb theme, better after all for an American than the themes chosen by Prescott and Ticknor and Motley, and precisely adapted to the pictorial and narrative powers of the soldier-minded, soldier-hearted author.

The quality which Parkman admired most in men — though he never seems to have loved men deeply, even his own heroes — was strength of will. That was the secret of his own power, and the sign, it must be added, of the limitations of this group of historians who came at the close of the golden age. Whatever a New England will can accomplish was wrought manfully by such admirable men as Prescott and Parkman. Trained intelligence, deliberate selection of subject, skillful cultivation of appropriate story-telling and picture-painting style, all these were theirs. But the "wild ecstasy" that thrilled the young Emerson as he crossed the bare Common at sunset, the "supernal beauty" of which Poe dreamed in the Fordham cottage, the bay horse and hound and turtle-dove which Thoreau lost long ago and could not find in his hut at Walden, these were something which our later Greeks of the New England Athens esteemed as foolishness.

CHAPTER VIII

ENTER now two egotists, who have little in common save their egotism, two outsiders who upset most of the conventional American rules for winning the literary race, two men of genius, in short, about whom we are still quarreling, and whose distinctive quality is more accurately perceived in Europe than it has ever been in the United States.

Both Poe and Whitman were Romanticists by temperament. Both shared in the tradition and influence of European Romanticism. But they were also late comers, and they were caught in the more morbid and extravagant phases of the great European movement while its current was beginning to ebb. Their acquaintance with its literature was mainly at second-hand and through the medium of British and American periodicals. Poe, who was older than Whitman by ten years, was fifteen when Byron died, in 1824. He was untouched by the nobler mood of Byron, though his verse was colored by the influence of Byron, Moore, and Shelley. His prose models were De Quincey, Disraeli, and Bulwer. Yet he owed more to Coleridge than to any of the Romantics. He was himself a sort of Coleridge without the piety, with the same keen penetrating critical intelligence, the same lovely opium-shadowed dreams, and, alas, with something of the same reputation as a dead-beat.

A child of strolling players, Poe happened to be born in Boston, but he hated "Frog-Pondium"—his favorite name for the city of his nativity—as much as Whistler hated his native town of Lowell. His father died early of tuberculosis, and his mother, after a pitiful struggle with disease and poverty, soon followed her husband to the grave. The boy, by physical inheritance a neurasthenic, though with marked bodily activity in youth, was adopted by the Allans, a kindly family in Richmond, Virginia. Poe liked to think of himself as a Southerner. He was sent to school in England, and in 1826, at seventeen, he attended for nearly a year the newly founded University of Virginia. He was a dark, short, bow-legged boy, with the

face of his own Roderick Usher.   He made a good
record in French and Latin, read, wrote and
recited poetry, tramped on the Ragged Mountains, and did not notably exceed his companions
in drinking and gambling.   But his Scotch foster-
father disapproved of his conduct and withdrew
him from the University.   A period of wandering
followed.   He enlisted in the army and was sta-
tioned in Boston in 1827, when his first volume,
Tamerlane, was published.   In 1829 he was in
Fortress Monroe, and published *Al Aaraf* at Baltimore.   He entered West Point in 1830, and was
surely, except Whistler, the strangest of all possible
cadets.   When he was dismissed in 1831, he had
written the marvellous lines *To Helen, Israfel,*
and *The City in the Sea.*   That is enough to have
in one's knapsack at the age of twenty-two.

In the eighteen years from 1831 to 1849, when
Poe's unhappy life came to an end in a Baltimore
hospital, his literary activity was chiefly that of a
journalist, critic, and short story writer.   He lived
in Baltimore, Richmond, Philadelphia, and New
York.   Authors who now exploit their fat bar-
gains with their publishers may have forgotten
that letter which Poe wrote back to Philadelphia
the morning after he arrived with his child-wife in

New York: "We are both in excellent spirits. . . . We have now got four dollars and a half left. To-morrow I am going to try and borrow three dollars, so that I may have a fortnight to go upon." When the child-wife died in the shabby cottage at Fordham, her wasted body was covered with the old army overcoat which Poe had brought from West Point. If Poe met some of the tests of practical life inadequately, it must be remembered that his health failed at twenty-five, that he was pitiably poor, and that the slightest indulgence in drink set his over-wrought nerves jangling. Ferguson, the former office-boy of the *Literary Messenger*, judged this man of letters with an office-boy's firm and experienced eye: "Mr. Poe was a fine gentleman when he was sober. He was ever kind and courtly, and at such times every-one liked him. But when he was drinking he was about one of the most disagreeable men I have ever met." "I am sorry for him," wrote C. F. Briggs to Lowell. "He has some good points, but taken altogether, he is badly made up." "Badly made up," no doubt, both in body and mind, but all respectable and prosperous Pharisees should be reminded that Poe did not make him-self; or rather, that he could not make himself

over. Very few men can. Given Poe's temperament, and the problem is insoluble. He wrote
to Lowell in 1844: "I have been too deeply conscious of the mutability and evanescence of tem-
poral things to give any continuous effort to
anything — to be consistent in anything. My life
has been *whim* — impulse — passion — a longing
for solitude — a scorn of all things present in an
earnest desire for the future." It is the pathetic
confession of a dreamer. Yet this dreamer was
also a keen analyzer, a tireless creator of beautiful
things. In them he sought and found a refuge
from actuality. The marvel of his career is, as I
have said elsewhere, that this solitary, embittered
craftsman, out of such hopeless material as nega-
tions and abstractions, shadows and superstitions,
out of disordered fancies and dreams of physical
horror and strange crime, should have wrought
structures of imperishable beauty.

Let us notice the critical instinct which he
brought to the task of creation. His theory of
verse is simple, in fact too simple to account for
all of the facts. The aim of poetry, according to
Poe, is not truth but pleasure — the rhythmical
creation of beauty. Poetry should be brief, indefi-
nite, and musical. Its chief instrument is sound.

A certain quaintness or grotesqueness of tone is a means for satisfying the thirst for supernal beauty. Hence the musical lyric is to Poe the only true type of poetry; a long poem does not exist. Readers who respond more readily to auditory than to visual or motor stimulus are therefore Poe's chosen audience. For them he executes, like Paganini, marvels upon his single string. He has easily recognizable devices: the dominant note, the refrain, the "repetend," that is to say the phrase which echoes, with some variation, a phrase or line already used. In such poems as *To Helen, Israfel, The Haunted Palace, Annabel Lee,* the theme, the tone, the melody all weave their magic spell; it is like listening to a lute-player in a dream.

That the device often turns into a trick is equally true. In *The Bells* and *The Raven* we detect the prestidigitator. It is jugglery, though such juggling as only a master-musician can perform. In *Ulalume* and other show-pieces the wires get crossed and the charm snaps, scattering tinsel fragments of nonsense verse. Such are the dangers of the technical temperament unenriched by wide and deep contact with human feeling.

Poe's theory of the art of the short story is

now familiar enough. The power of a tale, he
thought, turned chiefly if not solely upon its unity,
its harmony of effect. This is illustrated in all
of his finest stories. In *The Fall of the House of
Usher* the theme is Fear; the opening sentence
strikes the key and the closing sentence contains
the climax. In the whole composition every sentence is modulated to the one end in view. The
autumn landscape tones with the melancholy
house; the somber chamber frames the cadaverous
face of Roderick Usher; the face is an index of the
tumultuous agitation of a mind wrestling with
the grim phantom Fear and awaiting the cumulative horror of the final moment. In *Ligeia*,
which Poe sometimes thought the best of all his
tales, the theme is the ceaseless life of the will, the
potency of the spirit of the beloved and departed
woman. The unity of effect is absolute, the
workmanship consummate. So with the theme
of revenge in *The Cask of Amontillado*, the theme
of mysterious intrigue in *The Assignation*. In
Poe's detective stories, or tales of ratiocination as
he preferred to call them, he takes to pieces for
our amusement a puzzle which he has cunningly
put together. *The Gold Bug* is the best known of
these, *The Purloined Letter* the most perfect, *The*

Murders in the Rue Morgue the most sensational. Then there are the tales upon scientific subjects or displaying the pretence of scientific knowledge, where the narrator loves to pose as a man without imagination and with "habits of rigid thought." And there are tales of conscience, of which *The Black Cat* is the most fearful and *William Wilson* the most subtle; and there are landscape sketches and fantasies and extravaganzas, most of these poor stuff.

It is ungrateful and perhaps unnecessary to dwell upon Poe's limitations. His scornful glance caught certain aspects of the human drama with camera-like precision. Other aspects of life, and nobler, he never seemed to perceive. The human comedy sometimes moved him to laughter, but his humor is impish and his wit malign. His imagination fled from the daylight; he dwelt in the twilight among the tombs. He closed his eyes to dream, and could not see the green sunlit earth, seed-time and harvest, man going forth to his toil and returning to his hearthstone, the America that laughs as it labors. He wore upon his finger the magic ring and the genii did his bidding. But we could wish that the palaces they reared for him were not in such a

omber land, with such infernal lights gleaming
n their windows, and crowded with such horror-
aunted forms. We could wish that his imagin-
tion dealt less often with those primitive terrors
hat belong to the childhood of our race. Yet
vhen his spell is upon us we lapse back by a sort
f atavism into primal savagery and shudder with
recrudescence of long forgotten fears. No doubt
Poe was ignorant of life, in the highest sense. He
vas caged in by his ignorance. Yet he had beau-
iful dusky wings that bruised themselves against
is prison.

Poe was a tireless critic of his own work, and
both his standards of workmanship and his
critical precepts have been of great service to
is careless countrymen. He turned out between
four and five short stories a year, was poorly paid
or them, and indeed found difficulty in selling
hem at all. Yet he was constantly correcting
hem for the better. His best poems were likewise his latest. He was tantalized with the desire
or artistic perfection. He became the path-
breaker for a long file of men in France, Italy,
England, and America. He found the way and
they brought back the glory and the cash.

I have sometimes imagined Poe, with four other

men and one woman, seated at a dinner-table laid
for six, and talking of their art and of themselves.
What would the others think of Poe? I fancy
that Thackeray would chat with him courteously
but would not greatly care for him. George
Eliot, woman-like, would pity him. Hawthorne
would watch him with those inscrutable eyes and
understand him better than the rest. But Steven
son would be immensely interested; he would begin
an essay on Poe before he went to sleep. And
Mr. Kipling would look sharply at him: he has
seen that man before, in *The Gate of a Hundred
Sorrows*. All of them would find in him something to praise, a great deal to marvel at, and
perhaps not much to love. And the sensitive,
shabby, lonely Poe—what would he think of them?
He might not care much for the other guests, but I
think he would say to himself with a thrill of pride:
"I belong at this table." And he does.

Walt Whitman, whom his friend O'Connor
dubbed the "good gray poet," offers a bizarre
contrast to Edgar Allan Poe. There was nothing
distinctively American about Poe except his
ingenuity; he had no interest in American history
or in American ideas; he was a timeless, placeless
embodiment of technical artistry. But Whitman

had a passion for his native soil; he was hypnotized
by the word America; he spent much of his mature
life in brooding over the question, "What, after
all, is an American, and what should an American
poet be in our age of science and democracy?"
It is true that he was as untypical as Poe of the
average citizen of "these states." His personality is unique. In many respects he still baffles
our curiosity. He repels many of his countrymen
without arousing the pity which adds to their
romantic interest in Poe. Whatever our literary
students may feel, and whatever foreign critics
may assert, it must be acknowledged that to the
vast majority of American men and women "good
old Walt" is still an outsider.

Let us try to see first the type of mind with
which we are dealing. It is fundamentally religious, perceiving the unity and kinship and glory
of all created things. It is this passion of worship
which inspired St. Francis of Assisi's *Canticle to the
Sun*. It cries, "Benedicite, Omnia opera Domini:
All ye Green Things upon the Earth, bless ye the
Lord!" That is the real motto for Whitman's
Leaves of Grass. Like St. Francis, and like his
own immediate master, Ralph Waldo Emerson,
Whitman is a mystic. He cannot argue the

ultimate questions; he asserts them. Instead of marshaling and sifting the proofs for immortality, he chants "I know I am deathless." Like Emerson again, Whitman shares that peculiarly American type of mysticism known as Transcendentalism, but he came at the end of this movement instead of at the beginning of it. In his Romanticism, likewise, he is an end of an era figure. His affiliations with Victor Hugo are significant; and a volume of Scott's poems which he owned at the age of sixteen became his "inexhaustible mine and treasury for more than sixty years." Finally, and quite as uncompromisingly as Emerson, Thoreau, and Poe, Whitman is an individualist. He represents the assertive, Jacksonian period of our national existence. In a thousand similes he makes a declaration of independence for the separate person, the "single man" of Emerson's Phi Beta Kappa address. "I wear my hat as I please, indoors and out." Sometimes this is mere swagger. Sometimes it is superb.

So much for the type. Let us turn next to the story of Whitman's life. It must here be told in the briefest fashion, for Whitman's own prose and poetry relate the essentials of his biography. He was born on Long Island, of New England and

Dutch ancestry, in 1819. Lowell, W. W. Story, and Charles A. Dana were born in that year, as was also George Eliot. Whitman's father was a carpenter, who "leaned to the Quakers." There were many children. When little "Walt"—as he was called, to distinguish him from his father, Walter—was four, the family moved to Brooklyn. The boy had scanty schooling, and by the time he was twenty had tried type-setting, teaching, and editing a country newspaper on Long Island. He was a big, dark-haired fellow, sensitive, emotional, extraordinarily impressible.

The next sixteen years were full of happy vagrancy. At twenty-two he was editing a paper in New York, and furnishing short stories to the *Democratic Review*, a literary journal which numbered Bryant, Longfellow, Whittier, Poe, Hawthorne, and Thoreau among its contributors. He wrote a novel on temperance, "mostly in the reading-room of Tammany Hall," and tried here and there an experiment in free verse. He was in love with the pavements of New York and the Brooklyn ferry-boats, in love with Italian opera and with long tramps over Long Island. He left his position on *The Brooklyn Eagle* and wandered south to New Orleans. By and by he drifted back to New York, tried lecturing, worked at the carpenter's trade with his father, and brooded over a book—"a book of new things."

This was the famous *Leaves of Grass*. He set the type himself, in a Brooklyn printing-office, and printed about eight hundred copies. The book had a portrait of the author — a meditative, gray-bearded poet in workman's clothes — and a confused preface on America as a field for the true poet. Then followed the new gospel, "I celebrate myself," chanted in long lines of free verse, whose patterns perplexed contemporary readers. For the most part it was passionate speech rather than song, a rhapsodical declamation in hybrid rhythms. Very few people bought the book or pretended to understand what it was all about. Some were startled by the frank sexuality of certain poems. But Emerson wrote to Whitman from Concord: "I find it the most extraordinary piece of wit and wisdom that America has yet contributed."

Until the Civil War was half over, Whitman remained in Brooklyn, patiently composing new poems for successive printings of his book. Then he went to the front to care for a wounded brother, and finally settled down in a Washington garret to spend his strength as an army hospital nurse. He wrote *Drum Taps* and other magnificent poems about the War, culminating in his threnody on Lincoln's death, *When Lilacs last in the Dooryard Bloomed.* Swinburne called this "the most sonorous nocturn ever chanted in the church of the world." After the war had ended, Whitman stayed on in Washington as a government clerk, and saw much of John Burroughs and W. D. O'Connor. John Hay was a staunch friend. Some of the best known poets and critics of England and the Continent now began to recognize his genius. But his health had been permanently shattered by his heroic service as a nurse, and in 1873 he suffered a paralytic stroke which forced him to resign his position in Washington and remove to his brother's home in Camden, New Jersey.

He was only fifty-four, but his best work was already done, and his remaining years, until his death in 1892, were those of patient and serene invalidism. He wrote some fascinating prose in this final period, and his cluttered chamber in Camden became the shrine of many a literary pilgrim, among them some of the foremost men of letters of this country and of Europe. He was cared for by loyal friends. Occasionally he appeared in public, a magnificent gray figure of a man. And then, at seventy-three, the "Dark mother always gliding near" enfolded him.

There are puzzling things in the physical and moral constitution of Walt Whitman, and the obstinate questions involved in his theory of poetry and in his actual poetical performance are still far from solution. But a few points concerning him are by this time fairly clear. They must be swiftly summarized.

The first obstacle to the popular acceptance of Walt Whitman is the formlessness or alleged formlessness of *Leaves of Grass*. This is a highly technical question, involving a more accurate notation than has thus far been made of the patterns and tunes of free verse and of emotional prose. Whitman's "new and national declamatory expression," as he termed it, cannot receive a final technical valuation until we have made more scientific progress in the analysis of rhythms. As regards the contents of his verse, it is plain that he included much material unfused and untransformed by emotion. These elements foreign to the nature of poetry clog many of his lines. The enumerated objects in his catalogue or inventory poems often remain inert objects only. Like many mystics, he was hypnotized by external phenomena, and he often fails to communicate to his reader the trance-like emotion which he himself experienced. This imperfect transfusion of his material is a far more significant defect in Whitman's poetry than the relatively few passages of unashamed sexuality which shocked the American public in 1855.

The gospel or burden of *Leaves of Grass* is no more difficult of comprehension than the general drift of Emerson's essays, which helped to inspire it. The starting-point of the book is a mystical illumination regarding the unity and blessedness of the universe, an insight passing understanding, but based upon the revelatory experience of love. In the light of this experience, all created things are recognized as divine. The starting-point and center of the Whitman world is the individual man, the "strong person," imperturbable in mind, athletic in body, unconquerable, and immortal. Such individuals meet in comradeship, and pass together along the open roads of the world. No one is excluded because of his poverty or his sins; there is room in the ideal America for everybody except the doubter and sceptic. Whitman does not linger over the smaller groups of human society, like the family. He is not a fireside poet. He passes directly from his strong persons, meeting freely on the open road, to his conception of "these States." One of his typical visions of the breadth and depth and height of America will be found in *By Blue Ontario's Shore*. In this and in many similar rhapsodies Whitman holds obstinately to what may be termed the three points of his national creed. The first is the newness of America, and its expression is in his well-known chant of *Pioneers, O Pioneers*. Yet this new America is subtly related to the past; and in Whitman's later poems, such as *Passage to India*, the spiritual kinship of orient and occident is emphasized. The second article of the creed is the unity of America. Here he voices the conceptions of Hamilton, Clay, Webster, and Lincoln. In spite of all diversity in external aspects the republic is "one and indivisible." This unity, in Whitman's view, was cemented forever by the issue of the Civil War. Lincoln, the "Captain," dies indeed on the deck of the "victor ship," but the ship comes into the harbor "with object won." Third and finally, Whitman insists upon the solidarity of America with all countries of the globe. Particularly in his yearning and thoughtful old age, the poet perceived that humanity has but one heart and that it should have but one will. No American poet has ever prophesied so directly and powerfully concerning the final issue involved in that World War which he did not live to see.

Whitman, like Poe, had defects of character and defects of art. His life and work raise many problems which will long continue to fascinate and to baffle the critics. But after all of them have had their say, it will remain true that he was a seer and a prophet, far in advance of his own time, like Lincoln, and like Lincoln, an inspired interpreter of the soul of this republic.

CHAPTER IX

UNION AND LIBERTY

"THERE is what I call the American idea," declared Theodore Parker in the Anti-Slavery Convention of 1850. "This idea demands, as the proximate organization thereof, a democracy— that is, a government of all the people, by all the people, for all the people; of course, a government on the principle of eternal justice, the unchanging law of God; for shortness' sake, I will call it the idea of Freedom."

These are noble words, and they are thought to have suggested a familiar phrase of Lincoln's Gettysburg Address, thirteen years later. Yet students of literature, no less than students of politics, recognize the difficulty of summarizing in words a national "idea." Precisely what was the Greek "idea"? What is today the French "idea"? No single formula is adequate to express such a complex of fact, theories, moods — not even

206

the famous "Liberty, Fraternity, Equality."
The existence of a truly national life and literature
presupposes a certain degree of unity, an integration of race, language, political institutions, and
social ideals. It is obvious that this problem of
national integration meets peculiar obstacles in
the United States. Divergencies of race, tradition,
and social theory, and clashing interests of different sections have been felt from the beginning of
the nation's life. There was well-nigh complete
solidarity in the single province of New England
during a portion of the seventeenth century, and
under the leadership of the great Virginians there
was sufficient national fusion to make the Revolution successful. But early in the nineteenth
century, the opening of the new West, and the
increasing economic importance of Slavery as a
peculiar institution of the South, provoked again
the ominous question of the possibility of an enduring Union. From 1820 until the end of the Civil
War, it was the chief political issue of the United
States. The aim of the present chapter is to show
how the theme of Union and Liberty affected our
literature.

To appreciate the significance of this theme we
must remind ourselves again of what many per-

sons have called the civic note in our national writing. Franklin exemplified it in his day. It is far removed from the pure literary art of a Poe, a Hawthorne, a Henry James. It aims at action rather than beauty. It seeks to persuade, to convince, to bring things to pass. We shall observe it in the oratory of Clay and Webster, as they pleaded for compromise; in the editorials of Garrison, a foe to compromise and like Calhoun an advocate, if necessary, of disunion; in the epoch-making novel of Harriet Beecher Stowe; in the speeches of Wendell Phillips, in verse white-hot with political passion, and sermons blazing with the fury of attack and defense of principles dear to the human heart. We must glance, at least, at the lyrics produced by the war itself, and finally, we shall observe how Abraham Lincoln, the inheritor of the ideas of Jefferson, Clay, and Webster, perceives and maintains, in the noblest tones of our civic speech, the sole conditions of our continuance as a nation.

Let us begin with oratory, an American habit, and, as many besides Dickens have thought, an American defect. We cannot argue that question adequately here. It is sufficient to say that in the pioneer stages of our existence oratory was necessary as a stimulus to communal thought and feeling. The speeches of Patrick Henry and Samuel Adams were as essential to our winning independence as the sessions of statesmen and the armed conflicts in the field. And in that new West which came so swiftly and dramatically into existence at the close of the Revolution, the orator came to be regarded as the normal type of intellectual leadership. The stump grew more potent than schoolhouse and church and bench.

The very pattern, and, if one likes, the tragic victim of this glorification of oratory was Henry Clay, "Harry of the West," the glamour of whose name and the wonderful tones of whose voice became for a while a part of the political system of the United States. Union and Liberty were the master-passions of Clay's life, but the greater of these was Union. The half-educated young immigrant from Virginia hazarded his career at the outset by championing Anti-Slavery in the Kentucky Constitutional Convention; the last notable act of his life was his successful management, at the age of seventy-three, of the futile Compromise of 1850. All his life long he fought for national issues; for the War of 1812, for a protective tariff and an "American system," for the Missouri

Compromise of 1820 as a measure for national safety; and he had plead generously for the young South American republics and for struggling Greece. He had become the perpetual candidate of his party for the Presidency, and had gone down again and again in unforeseen and heart-rending defeat. Yet he could say honorably: "If any one desires to know the leading and paramount object of my public life, the preservation of this union will furnish him the key." One could wish that the speeches of this fascinating American were more readable today. They seem thin, facile, full of phrases — such adroit phrases as would catch the ear of a listening, applauding audience. Straight, hard thinking was not the road to political preferment in Clay's day. Calhoun had that power, as Lincoln had it. Webster had the capacity for it, although he was too indolent to employ his great gifts steadily. Yet it was Webster who analyzed kindly and a little sadly, for he was talking during Clay's last illness and just before his own, his old rival's defect in literary quality: "He was never a man of books. . . . I could never imagine him sitting comfortably in his library and reading quietly out of the great books of the past. He has been too fond of excitement — he has lived upon it;

he has been too fond of company, not enough alone; and has had few resources within himself." Were the limitations of a typical oratorical temperament ever touched more unerringly than in these words?

When Webster himself thundered, at the close of his reply to Hayne in 1830, "Union *and* Liberty, now and forever, one and inseparable," the words sank deeper into the consciousness of the American people than any similar sentiment uttered by Henry Clay. For Webster's was the richer, fuller nature, nurtured by "the great books of the past," brooding, as Lincoln was to brood later, over the seemingly insoluble problem of preserving a union of States half slave, half free. On the fateful seventh of March, 1850, Webster, like Clay, cast the immense weight of his personality and prestige upon the side of compromise. It was the ruin of his political fortune, for the mood of the North was changing, and the South preferred other candidates for the Presidency. Yet the worst that can fairly be said against that speech today is that it lacked moral imagination to visualize, as Mrs. Stowe was soon to visualize, the human results of slavery. As a plea for the transcendent necessity of maintaining the old Union it was consistent with Webster's whole development of political thought.

What were the secrets of that power that held Webster's hearers literally spellbound, and made the North think of him, after that alienation of 1850, as a fallen angel? No one can say fully, for we touch here the mysteries of personality and of the spoken word. But enough survives from the Webster legend, from his correspondence and political and legal oratory, to bring us into the presence of a superman. The dark Titan face, painted by such masters as Carlyle, Hawthorne, and Emerson; the magical voice, remembered now but by a few old men; the bodily presence, with its leonine suggestion of sleepy power only half put forth—these aided Webster to awe men or allure them into personal idolatry. Yet outside of New England he was admired rather than loved. There is still universal recognition of the mental capacity of this foremost lawyer and foremost statesman of his time. He was unsurpassed in his skill for direct, simple, limpid statement; but he could rise at will to a high Roman stateliness of diction, a splendid sonorousness of cadence. His greatest public appearances were in the Dartmouth College Case before the Supreme Court, the Plymouth,

Bunker Hill, and Adams–Jefferson commemorative orations, the Reply to Hayne, and the Seventh of March speeches in the Senate. Though he exhibited in his private life something of the prodigal recklessness of the pioneer, his mental operations were conservative, constructive. His life-long antagonist Calhoun declared that "The United States are not a nation." Webster, in opposition to this theory of a confederation of states, devoted his superb talents to the demonstration of the thesis that the United States "*is*," not "*are*." Thus he came to be known as the typical expounder of the Constitution. When he reached, in 1850, the turning-point of his career, his countrymen knew by heart his personal and political history, the New Hampshire boyhood and education, the rise to mastery at the New England bar, the service in the House of Representatives and the Senate and as Secretary of State. His speeches were already in the schoolbooks, and for twenty years boys had been declaiming his arguments against nullification. He had helped to teach America to think and to feel. Indeed it was through his oratory that many of his fellow-citizens had gained their highest conception of the beauty, the potency, and the dignity of human speech. And in truth he never exhibited his logical power and demonstrative skill more superbly than in the plea of the seventh of March for the preservation of the *status quo*, for the avoidance of mutual recrimination between North and South, for obedience to the law of the land. It was his supreme effort to reconcile an irreconcilable situation.

It failed, as we know. Whittier, Emerson, Theodore Parker, and indeed most of the voters of New England, believed that Webster had bartered his private convictions in the hope of securing the Presidential nomination in 1852. They assailed him savagely, and Webster died, a broken man, in the autumn of the Presidential year. "I have given my life to law and politics," he wrote to Professor Silliman. "Law is uncertain and politics are utterly vain." The dispassionate judgment of the present hour frees him from the charge of conscious treachery to principle. He was rather a martyr to his own conception of the obligations imposed by nationality. When these obligations run counter to human realities, the theories of statesmen must give way. Emerson could not refute that logic of Webster's argument for the Fugitive Slave Law, but he could at least record

WENDELL PHILLIPS

Photograph by Black, Boston.

HARRIET BEECHER STOWE, 1853

After the drawing by George Richmond.

CHARLES SUMNER

Photograph from the collection of L. C. Handy, Washington.

WENDELL PHILLIPS
Photograph by Black, Boston.

HARRIET BEECHER STOWE, 1853
After the drawing by George Richmond.

CHARLES SUMNER
Photograph from the collection of I. C. Handy, Washington.

in his private *Journal:* "*I will not obey it, by God!*"
So said hundreds of thousands of obscure men in
the North, but Webster did not or could not hear
them.

While no other orator of that period was so richly
endowed as Daniel Webster, the struggle for Union
and Liberty enlisted on both sides many eloquent
men. John C. Calhoun's acute, ingenious, masterly political theorizing can still be studied in
speeches that have lost little of their effectiveness
through the lapse of time. The years have dealt
roughly with Edward Everett, once thought to be
the pattern of oratorical gifts and graces. In
commemorative oratory, indeed, he ranked with
Webster, but the dust is settling upon his learned
and ornate pages. Rufus Choate, another conservative Whig in politics, and a leader, like Wirt
and Pinkney, at the bar, had an exotic, almost
Oriental fancy, a gorgeousness of diction, and an
intensity of emotion unrivaled among his contemporaries. His Dartmouth College eulogy of
Webster in 1853 shows him at his best. The Anti-
Slavery orators, on the other hand, had the ad-
vantage of a specific moral issue in which they led
the attack. Wendell Phillips was the most pol-
ished, the most consummate in his air of informal-

ity, and his example did much to puncture the American tradition of high-flown oratory. He was an expert in virulent denunciation, passionately unfair beneath his mask of conversational decorum, an aristocratic demagogue. He is still distrusted and hated by the Brahmin class of his own city, still adored by the children and grandchildren of slaves. Charles Sumner, like Edward Everett, seems sinking into popular oblivion, in spite of the statues and portraits and massive volumes of erudite and caustic and high-minded orations. He may be seen at his best in such books as Longfellow's *Journal and Correspondence* and the *Life and Letters* of George Ticknor. There one has a pleasant picture of a booklover, traveler, and friend. But in his public speech he was arrogant, unsympathetic, domineering. "Sumner is my idea of a bishop," said Lincoln tentatively. There are bishops and bishops, however, and if Henry Ward Beecher, whom Lincoln and hosts of other Americans admired, had only belonged to the Church of England, what an admirable Victorian bishop he might have made! Perhaps his best service to the cause of union was rendered by his speeches in England, where he fairly mobbed the mob and won them by his wit, courage, and by his appeal to the instinct of fair play. Beecher's oratory, in and out of the pulpit, was temperamental, sentimental in the better sense, and admirably human in all its instincts. He had an immense following, not only in political and humanitarian fields, but as a lovable type of the everyday American who can say undisputed things not only solemnly, if need be, but by preference with an infectious smile. The people who loved Mr. Beecher are the people who understand Mr. Bryan.

Foremost among the journalists of the great debate were William Lloyd Garrison and Horace Greeley. Garrison was a perfect example of the successful journalist as described by Zola — the man who keeps on pounding at a single idea until he has driven it into the head of the public. Everyone knows at least the sentence from his salutatory editorial in *The Liberator* on January 1, 1831: "I am in earnest—I will not retreat a single inch— *And I will be heard.*" He kept this vow, and he also kept the accompanying and highly characteristic promise: "I will be as harsh as truth and as uncompromising as justice. On this subject, I do not wish to think, or write, or speak, with moderation." But there would be little political literature in the world if its production were entrusted to the moderate type of man, and the files of *The Liberator*, though certainly harsh and full of all uncharitableness towards slave-owners, make excellent reading for the twentieth century American who perceives that in spite of the triumph of emancipation, in which Garrison had his fair share of glory, many aspects of our race-problem remain unsolved. Horace Greeley, the founder and editor of the *New York Tribune*, was a farmer's boy who learned early to speak and write the vocabulary of the plain people. Always interested in new ideas, even in Transcendentalism and Fourierism, his courage and energy and journalistic vigor gave him leadership in the later phases of the movement for enfranchisement. He did not hesitate to offer unasked advice to Lincoln on many occasions, and Lincoln enriched our literature by his replies. Greeley had his share of faults and fatuities, but in his best days he had an impressively loyal following among both rural and city-bred readers of his paper, and he remains one of the best examples of that obsolescent personal journalism which is destined to disappear under modern conditions of newspaper production. Readers really used to care for "what Greeley said" and

"Dana said" and "Sam Bowles said," and all of these men, with scores of others, have left their stamp upon the phrases and the tone of our political writing.

In the concrete issue of Slavery, however, it must be admitted that the most remarkable literary victory was scored, not by any orator or journalist, but by an almost unknown little woman, the author of *Uncle Tom's Cabin*. No American novel has had so curious a history and so great or so immediate an influence in this country and in Europe. In spite of all that has been written about it, its author's purpose is still widely misunderstood, particularly in the South, and the controversy over this one epoch-making novel has tended to obscure the literary reputation which Mrs. Stowe won by her other books.

Harriet Beecher, the daughter and the sister of famous clergymen, was born in Litchfield, Connecticut, in 1811. For seventeen years, from 1832 to 1849, she lived in the border city of Cincinnati, within sight of slave territory, and in daily contact with victims of the slave system. While her sympathies, like those of her father Lyman Beecher, were anti-slavery, she was not an Abolitionist in the Garrisonian sense of that word. At twenty-five she had married a widowed professor, Calvin Stowe, to whom she bore many children. She had written a few sketches of New England life, and her family thought her a woman of genius. Such was the situation in the winter of 1849–1850, when the Stowes migrated to Brunswick, Maine, where the husband had been appointed to a chair at Bowdoin. Pitiably poor, and distracted by household cares which she had to face single-handed— for the Professor was a "feckless body"—Mrs. Stowe nevertheless could not be indifferent to the national crisis over the Fugitive Slave Law. She had seen its working. When her sister-in-law wrote to her: "If I could use a pen as you can, I would write something that would make this whole nation feel what an accursed thing slavery is," Mrs. Stowe exclaimed: "God helping me, I will write something; I will if I live."

Uncle Tom's Cabin, begun in the spring of 1850, was a woman's answer to Webster's seventh of March speech. Its object was plainly stated to be "to awaken sympathy and feeling for the African race; to show their wrongs and sorrows, under a system so necessarily cruel and unjust as to defeat and do away the good effects of all that can be attempted for them, by their best friends under it." The book was permeated with what we now call the 1848 anti-aristocratic sentiment, the direct heritage of the French Revolution. "There is a *dies iræ* coming on, sooner or later," admits St. Clare in the story. "The same thing is working, in Europe, in England, and in this country." There was no sectional hostility in Mrs. Stowe's heart. "The people of the free states have defended, encouraged, and participated [in slavery]; and are more guilty for it, before God, than the South, in that they have *not* the apology of education or custom. If the mothers of the free states had all felt as they should in times past, the sons of the free states would not have been the holders, and proverbially the hardest masters, of slaves; the sons of the free states would not have connived at the extension of slavery in our national body." "Your book is going to be the great pacificator," wrote a friend of Mrs. Stowe; "it will unite North and South." But the distinctly Christian and fraternal intention of the book was swiftly forgotten in the storm of controversy that followed its appearance. It had been written hastily, fervidly, in the intervals of domestic toil at Brunswick, had been printed as a serial in *The National Era* without attracting much attention, and was issued in book form in March, 1852. Its sudden and amazing success was not confined to this country. The story ran in three Paris newspapers at once, was promptly dramatized, and has held the stage in France ever since. It was placed upon the *Index* in Italy, as being subversive of established authority. Millions of copies were sold in Europe, and *Uncle Tom's Cabin*, more than any other cause, held the English working men in sympathy with the North in the English cotton crisis of our Civil War.

It is easy to see the faults of this masterpiece and impossible not to recognize its excellencies. "If our art has not scope enough to include a book of this kind," said Madame George Sand, "we had better stretch the terms of our art a little." For the book proved to be, as its author had hoped, a "living dramatic reality." Topsy, Chloe, Sam and Andy, Miss Ophelia and Legree are alive. Mrs. St. Clare might have been one of Balzac's indolent, sensuous women. Uncle Tom himself is a bit too good to be true, and readers no longer weep over the death of little Eva — nor, for that matter, over the death of Dickens's little Nell. There is some melodrama, some religiosity, and there are some absurd recognition scenes at the close. Nevertheless with an instinctive genius which Zola would have envied, Mrs. Stowe embodies in men and women the vast and ominous system of slavery. All the tragic forces of necessity, blindness, sacrifice, and retribution are here: neither Shelby, nor Eliza, nor the tall Kentuckian who aids her, nor John Bird, nor Uncle Tom himself in the final act of his drama, can help himself. For good or evil they are the products and results of the system; and yet they have and they give the illusion of volition.

Mrs. Stowe lived to write many another novel and short story, among them *Dred, The Minister's Wooing, Oldtown Folks, Oldtown Fireside Stories.* In the local short story she deserves the honors due to one of the pioneers, and her keen affectionate observation, her humor, and her humanity, would have given her a literary reputation quite independent of her masterpiece. But she is likely to pay the penalty of that astounding success, and to go down to posterity as the author of a single book. She would not mind this fate.

The poetry of the idea of Freedom and of the sectional struggle which was necessary before that idea could be realized in national policy is on the whole not commensurate with the significance of the issue itself. Any collection of American political verse produced during this period exhibits spirited and sincere writing, but the combination of mature literary art and impressive general ideas is comparatively rare. There are single poems of Whittier, Lowell, and Whitman which meet every test of effective political and social verse, but the main body of poetry, both sectional and national, written during the thirty years ending with 1865 lacks breadth, power, imaginative daring. The continental spaciousness and energy which foreign critics thought they discovered in Whitman is not characteristic of our poetry as a whole. Victor Hugo and Shelley and Swinburne have written far more magnificent republican poetry than ours. The passion for freedom has been very real upon this side of the Atlantic; it pulsed in the local loyalty of the men who sang *Dixie* as well as in their antagonists who chanted *John Brown's Body* and *The Battle Hymn of the Republic;* but this passion has not yet lifted and ennobled any notable mass of American verse. Even the sentiment of union was more adequately voiced in editorials and sermons and orations, even in a short story — Edward Everett Hale's *Man Without a Country* — than by most of the poets who attempted to glorify that theme.

Nevertheless the verse of these thirty years is rich in provincial and sectional loyalties. It has earnestness and pathos. We have, indeed, no adequate national anthem, even yet, for neither the words nor the music of *The Star-Spangled Banner* fully express what we feel while we are trying to sing it, as the *Marseillaise*, for example, does express the very spirit of revolutionary republicanism. But in true pioneer fashion we get along with a makeshift until something better turns up. The lyric and narrative verse of the Civil War itself was great in quantity, and not more inferior in quality than the war verse of other nations has often proved to be when read after the immediate occasion for it has passed. Single lyrics by Timrod and Paul Hayne, Boker, H. H. Brownell, Read, Stedman, and other men are still full of fire. Yet Mrs. Howe's *Battle Hymn*, scribbled hastily in the gray dawn, interpreted, as no other lyric of the war quite succeeded in interpreting, the mystical glory of sacrifice for Freedom. Soldiers sang it in camp; women read it with tears; children repeated it in school, vaguely but truly perceiving in it, as their fathers had perceived in Webster's *Reply to Hayne* thirty years before, the idea of union made "simple, sensuous, passionate." No American

15

poem has had a more dramatic and intense life in the quick breathing imagination of men.

More and more, however, the instinct of our people is turning to the words of Abraham Lincoln as the truest embodiment in language, as his life was the truest embodiment in action, of our national ideal. It is a curious reversal of contemporary judgments that thus discovers in the homely phrases of a frontier lawyer the most perfect literary expression of the deeper spirit of his time. "How knoweth this man letters, having never learned?" asked the critical East. The answer is that he had learned in a better school than the East afforded. The story of Lincoln's life is happily too familiar to need retelling here, but some of the elements in his growth in the mastery of speech may at least be summarized.

Lincoln had a slow, tireless mind, capable of intense concentration. It was characteristic of him that he rarely took notes when trying a law case, saying that the notes distracted his attention. When his partner Herndon was asked when Lincoln had found time to study out the constitutional history of the United States, Herndon expressed the opinion that it was when Lincoln was lying on his back on the office sofa, apparently watching the flies upon the ceiling. This combination of bodily repose with intense mental and spiritual activity is familiar to those who have studied the biography of some of the great mystics. Walter Pater pointed it out in the case of Wordsworth.

In recalling the poverty and restriction of Lincoln's boyhood and his infrequent contact with schoolhouses, it is well to remember that he managed nevertheless to read every book within twenty miles of him. These were not many, it is true, but they included *The Bible, Æsop's Fables, Pilgrim's Progress, Robinson Crusoe*, and, a little later, Burns and Shakespeare. Better food than this for the mind of a boy has never been found. Then he came to the history of his own country since the Declaration of Independence and mastered it. "I am tolerably well acquainted with the history of the country," he remarked in his Chicago speech of 1858; and in the Cooper Union speech of 1860 he exhibited a familiarity with the theory and history of the Constitution which amazed the young lawyers who prepared an annotated edition of the address. "He has wit, facts, dates," said Douglas, in extenuation of his own disinclination to enter upon the famous joint debates, and, when Douglas returned to Washington after the debates were over, he confessed to the young Henry Watterson that "he is the greatest debater I have ever met, either here or anywhere else." Douglas had won the senatorship and could afford to be generous, but he knew well enough that his opponent's facts and dates had been unanswerable. Lincoln's mental grip, indeed, was the grip of a born wrestler. "I've got him," he had exclaimed toward the end of the first debate, and the Protean Little Giant, as Douglas was called, had turned and twisted in vain, caught by "that long-armed creature from Illinois." He could indeed win the election of 1858, but he had been forced into an interpretation of the Dred Scott decision which cost him the Presidency in 1860.

Lincoln's keen interest in words and definitions, his patience in searching the dictionary, is known to every student of his life. Part of his singular discrimination in the use of language is due to his legal training, but his style was never professionalized. Neither did it have anything of that frontier glibness and banality which was the curse of popular oratory in the West and South. Words were weapons in the hands of this self-taught fighter for ideas: he kept their edges sharp, and could if necessary use them with deadly accuracy. He framed the "Freeport dilemma" for the unwary feet of Douglas as cunningly as a fox-hunter lays his trap. "Gentlemen," he had said of an earlier effort, "Judge Douglas informed you that this speech of mine was probably carefully prepared. *I admit that it was.*"

The story, too, was a weapon of attack and defense for this master fabulist. Sometimes it was a readier mode of argument than any syllogism; sometimes it gave him, like the traditional diplomatist's pinch of snuff, an excuse for pausing while he studied his adversary or made up his own mind; sometimes, with the instinct of a poetic soul, he invented a parable and gravely gave it a historic setting "over in Sangamon County." For although upon his intellectual side the man was a subtle and severe logician, on his emotional side he was a lover of the concrete and human. He was always, like John Bunyan, dreaming and seeing "a man" who symbolized something apposite to the occasion. Thus even his invented stories aided his marvelous capacity for statement, for specific illustration of a general law. Lincoln's destiny was to be that of an explainer, at first to a local audience in store or tavern or courtroom, then to upturned serious faces of Illinois farmers who wished to hear national issues made clear to them, then to a listening nation in the agony of civil war, and ultimately to a world which looks to Lincoln as an exponent and interpreter of the essence of democracy.

As the audience increased, the style took on beauty and breadth, as if the man's soul were looking through wider and wider windows at the world. But it always remained the simplest of styles. In an offhand reply to a serenade by an Indiana regiment, or in answering a visiting deputation of clergymen at the White House, Lincoln could summarize and clarify a complicated national situation with an ease and orderliness and fascination that are the despair of professional historians. He never wasted a word. "Go to work is the only cure for your case," he wrote to John D. Johnston. There are ten words in that sentence and none of over four letters. The *Gettysburg Address* contains but two hundred and seventy words, in ten sentences. "It is a flat failure," said Lincoln despondently; but Edward Everett, who had delivered "the" oration of that day, wrote to the President: "I should be glad if I could flatter myself that I came as near to the central idea of

WILLIAM DEAN HOWELLS

Photograph.

SAMUEL L. CLEMENS, "MARK TWAIN"

Photograph by Sarony, New York.

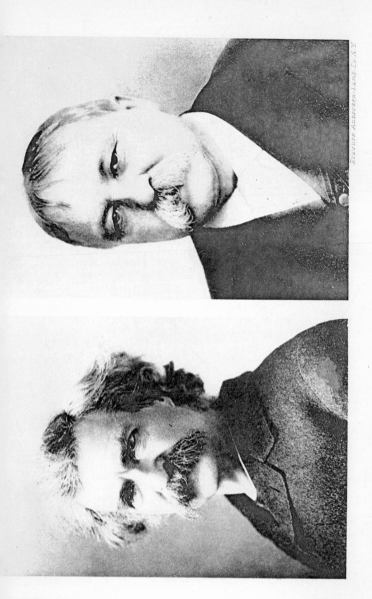

the occasion in two hours as you did in two minutes." Today the *Address* reads as if Lincoln knew that it would ultimately be stamped in bronze.

Yet the real test of Lincoln's supremacy in our distinctly civic literature lies not so much in his skill in the manipulation of language, consummate as that was, but rather in those large elements of his nature which enabled him to perceive the true quality and ideal of American citizenship and its significance to the world. There was melancholy in that nature, else there had been a less rich humor; there was mysticism and a sense of religion which steadily deepened as his responsibilities increased. There was friendliness, magnanimity, pity for the sorrowful, patience for the slow of brain and heart, and an expectation for the future of humanity which may best be described in the old phrase "waiting for the Kingdom of God." His recurrent dream of the ship coming into port under full sail, which preluded many important events in his own life — he had it the night before he was assassinated — is significant not only of that triumph of a free nation which he helped to make possible, but also of the victory of what he loved to call "the whole family of man."

"That is the real issue," he had declared in closing the debates with Douglas; "that is the issue that will continue in this country when these poor tongues of Judge Douglas and myself shall be silent. It is the eternal struggle between these two principles — right and wrong — throughout the world. They are the two principles that have stood face to face from the beginning of time; and will ever continue to struggle. The one is the common right of humanity, and the other the divine right of kings."

For this representative Anglo-Saxon man, developed under purely American conditions, maturing slowly, keeping close to facts, dying, like the old English saint, while he was "still learning," had none of the typical hardness and selfishness of the Anglo-Saxon. A brooder and idealist, he was one of those "prophetic souls of the wide world dreaming on things to come," with sympathies and imagination that reached out beyond the immediate urgencies of his race and nation to comprehend the universal task and discipline of the sons of men. In true fraternity and democracy this Westerner was not only far in advance of his own day, but he is also far in advance of ours which raises statues to his memory. Yet he was used to loneliness and to the long view, and even across the welter of the World War of the twentieth century Lincoln would be tall enough to see that ship coming into the harbor under full sail.

CHAPTER X

A NEW NATION

THE changes that have come over the inner spirit and the outward expression of American life since Lincoln's day are enough to startle the curiosity of the dullest observer. Yet they have been accomplished within the lifetime of a single man of letters. The author of one of the many campaign biographies of Lincoln in 1860 was William Dean Howells, then an Ohio journalist of twenty-three. In 1917, at the age of eighty, Mr. Howells is still adding to his long row of charming and memorable books. Every phase of American writing since the middle of the last century has fallen under the keen and kindly scrutiny of this loyal follower of the art of literature. As producer, editor, critic, and friend of the foremost writers of his epoch, Mr. Howells has known the books of our new national era as no one else could have known them. Some future historian of the period may piece together, from no other sources than Mr. Howells's writings, an unrivaled picture of our book-making during more than sixty years. All that the present historian can attempt is to sketch with bungling fingers a few men and a few tendencies which seem to characterize the age.

One result of the Civil War was picturesquely set forth in Emerson's *Journal*. The War had unrolled a map of the Union, he said, and hung it in every man's house. There was a universal shifting of attention, if not always from the province or section to the image of the nation itself, at least a shift of focus from one section to another. The clash of arms had meant many other things besides the triumph of Union and the freedom of the slaves. It had brought men from every state into rude jostling contact with one another and had developed a new social and human curiosity. It may serve as another illustration of Professor Shaler's law of tension and release. The one overshadowing issue which had absorbed so much thought and imagination and energy had suddenly disappeared. Other shadows were to gather, of course. Reconstruction of the South was one of them, and the vast economic and industrial changes that followed the opening of the New West were to bring fresh problems almost as intricate as the question of slavery had been. But for the moment no one thought of these things. The South accepted defeat as superbly as she had fought, and began to plough once more. The jubilant North went back to work—to build transcontinental railroads, to organize great industries, and to create new states.

The significant American literature of the first decade after the close of the War is not in the books dealing directly with themes involved in the War itself. It is rather the literature of this new release of energy, the new curiosity as to hitherto unknown sections, the new humor and romance. Fred Lewis Pattee, the author of an admirable *History of American Literature since 1870*, uses scarcely too strong a phrase when he entitles this period "The Second Discovery of America"; and he quotes effectively from Mark Twain, who was himself one of these discoverers: "The eight years in America from 1860 to 1868 uprooted institutions that were centuries old, changed the politics of a people, transformed the social life of half the country, and wrought so profoundly upon the entire national character that the influence cannot be measured short of two or three generations."

Let us begin with the West, and with that joyous stage-coach journey of young Samuel L. Clemens across the plains to Nevada in 1861, which he describes in *Roughing It*. Who was this Argonaut of the new era, and what makes him representative of his countrymen in the epoch of release? Born in Missouri in 1835, the son of an impractical emigrant from Virginia, the youth had lived from his fourth until his eighteenth year on the banks of the Mississippi. He had learned the printer's trade, had wandered east and back again, had served for four years as a river-pilot on the Mississippi, and had tried to enter the Confederate army. Then came the six crowded years, chiefly as newspaper reporter, in the boom times of Nevada and California. His fame began with the publication in New York in 1867 of *The Celebrated Jumping Frog of Calaveras County*. A newspaper now sent him to Europe to record "what he sees with his own eyes." He did so in *Innocents Abroad*, and his countrymen shouted with laughter. This, then, was "Europe" after all — another "fake" until this shrewd river-pilot who signed himself "Mark Twain" took its soundings! Then came a series of far greater books—*Roughing It, Life on the Mississippi, The Gilded Age* (in collaboration), and *Tom Sawyer* and *Huckleberry Finn* — books that make our American *Odyssey*, rich in the spirit of romance and revealing the magic of the great river as no other pages can ever do again. Gradually Mark Twain became a public character; he retrieved on the lecture platform the loss of a fortune earned by his books; he enjoyed his honorary D. Litt. from Oxford University. Every reader of American periodicals came to recognize the photographs of that thick shock of hair, those heavy eyebrows, the gallant drooping little figure, the striking clothes, the inevitable cigar: all these things seemed to go with the part of professional humorist, to be like the caressing drawl of Mark's voice. The force of advertisement could no further go. But at bottom he was far other than a mere maker of boisterous jokes for people with frontier preferences in humor. He was a passionate, chivalric lover of things fair and good, although too honest to pretend to see beauty and goodness where he could not personally detect them — and an equally passionate hater of evil. Read *The Man Who Corrupted Hadleyburg* and *The Mysterious Stranger*. In his last years, torn by private sorrows, he turned as black a philosophical pessimist as we have bred. He died at

his new country seat in Connecticut in 1910.   Mr.
Paine has written his life in three great volumes,
and there is a twenty-five volume edition of his
Works.

All the evidence seems to be in.   Yet the verdict of the public seems not quite made up.   It
is clear that Mark Twain the writer of romance is
gaining upon Mark Twain the humorist.   The
inexhaustible American appetite for frontier types
of humor seizes upon each new variety, crunches
it with huge satisfaction, and then tosses it away.
John Phoenix, Josh Billings, Jack Downing, Bill
Arp, Petroleum V. Nasby, Artemus Ward, Bill
Nye — these are already obsolescent names.   If
Clemens lacked something of Artemus Ward's
whimsical delicacy and of Josh Billings's tested
human wisdom, he surpassed all of his competitors
in a certain rude, healthy masculinity, the humor of
river and mining-camp and printing-office, where
men speak without censorship.   His country-men
liked exaggeration, and he exaggerated; they
liked irreverence, and he had turned iconoclast
in *Innocents Abroad.*   As a professional humorist,
he has paid the obligatory tax for his extravagance, over-emphasis, and undisciplined taste, but
such faults are swiftly forgotten when one turns

to Huckleberry Finn and the negro Jim and Pudd'n-head Wilson, when one feels Mark Twain's power in sheer description and episode, his magic in evoking landscape and atmosphere, his blazing scorn at injustice and cruelty, his contempt for quacks.

Bret Harte, another discoverer of the West, wears less well than Mark Twain as a personal figure, but has a sure place in the evolution of the American short story, and he did for the mining-camps of California what Clemens wrought for the Mississippi River: he became their profane poet. Yet he was never really of them. He was the clever outsider, with a prospector's eye, looking for literary material, and finding a whole rich mine of it—a bigger and richer, in fact, than he was really qualified to work. But he located a golden vein of it with an instinct that did credit to his dash of Hebrew blood. Born in Albany, a teacher's son, brought up on books and in many cities, Harte emigrated to California in 1854 at the age of sixteen. He became in turn a drug-clerk, teacher, type-setter, editor, and even Secretary of the California Mint — his nearest approach, apparently, to the actual work of the mines. In 1868, while editor of *The Overland Monthly*, he wrote the short story which was destined to make him famous in the East and to release him from California forever. It was *The Luck of Roaring Camp*. He had been writing romantic sketches in prose and verse for years; he had steeped himself in Dickens, like everybody else in the eighteen-sixties; and now he saw his pay-gravel shining back into his own shining eyes. It was a pocket, perhaps, rather than a lead, but Bret Harte worked to the end of his career this material furnished by the camps, this method of the short story. He never returned to California after his joyous exit in 1871. For a few years he tried living in New York, but from 1878 until his death in 1902 Bret Harte lived in Europe, still turning out California stories for an English and American public which insisted upon that particular pattern.

That the pattern was arbitrary, theatrical, sentimental, somewhat meretricious in design, in a word insincere like its inventor, has been repeated at due intervals ever since 1868. The charge is true; yet it is far from the whole truth concerning Bret Harte's artistry. In mastery of the technique of the short story he is fairly comparable with Poe, though less original, for it was Poe who formulated, when Bret Harte was a child

16

of six, the well-known theory of the unity of effect of the brief tale. This unity Harte secured through a simplification, often an insulation, of his theme, the omission of quarreling details, an atmosphere none the less novel for its occasional theatricality, and characters cunningly modulated to the one note they were intended to strike. *Tennessee's Partner*, *The Outcast of Poker Flat*, and all the rest are triumphs of selective skill — as bright nuggets as ever glistened in the pan at the end of a hard day's labor. That they do not adequately represent the actual California of the fifties, as old Californians obstinately insist, is doubtless true, but it is beside the point. Here is no Tolstoi painting the soul of his race in a few pages: Harte is simply a disciple of Poe and Dickens, turning the Poe construction trick gracefully, with Dickensy characters and consistently romantic action.

The West has been rediscovered many a time since that decade which witnessed the first literary bonanza of Mark Twain and Bret Harte. It will continue to be discovered, in its fresh sources of appeal to the imagination, as long as Plains and Rockies and Coast endure, as long as there is any glow upon a distant horizon. It is

not places that lose romantic interest: the imme-
morial English counties and the Bay of Naples
offer themselves freely to the artist, generation after
generation.   What is lost is the glamour of youth,
the specific atmosphere of a given historical epoch.
Colonel W. F. Cody ("Buffalo Bill") has typified
to millions of American boys the great period of
the Plains, with its Indian fighting, its slaughter of
buffaloes, its robbing of stage-coaches, its superb
riders etched against the sky.   But the Wild
West was retreating, even in the days of Daniel
Boone and Davy Crockett.   The West of the cow-
boys, as Theodore Roosevelt and Owen Wister
knew it and wrote of it in the eighties and nineties,
has disappeared, though it lives on in fiction and
on the screen.

Jack London, born in California in 1876, was
forced to find his West in Alaska — and in alcohol.
He was what he and his followers liked to call the
virile or red-blooded type, responsive to the " Call
of the Wild," "living life naked and tensely."   In
his talk Jack London was simple and boyish, with
plenty of humor over his own literary and social
foibles.   His books are very uneven, but he wrote
many a hard-muscled, clean-cut page.   If the Bret
Harte theory of the West was that each man is at

bottom a sentimentalist, Jack London's formula was that at bottom every man is a brute. Each theory gave provender enough for a short-story writer to carry on his back, but is hardly adequate, by itself, for a very long voyage over human life.

"Joaquin" (Cincinnatus Heine) Miller, who was born in 1841 and died in 1913, had even less of a formula for the West than Jack London. He was a word-painter of its landscapes, a rider over its surfaces. Cradled "in a covered wagon pointing West," mingling with wild frontier life from Alaska to Nicaragua, miner, Indian fighter, hermit, poseur in London and Washington, then hermit again in California, the author of *Songs of the Sierras* at least knew his material. Byron, whom he adored and imitated, could have invented nothing more romantic than Joaquin's life; but though Joaquin inherited Scotch intensity, he had nothing of the close mental grip of the true Scot and nothing of his humor. Vast stretches of his poetry are empty; some of it is grandiose, elemental, and yet somehow artificial, as even the Grand Canyon itself looks at certain times.

John Muir, another immigrant Scot who reached California in 1868, had far more stuff in him than Joaquin Miller. He had studied geology, botany, and chemistry at the new University of Wisconsin, and then for years turned explorer of forests, peaks, and glaciers, not writing, at first, except in his *Journal*, but forever absorbing and worshiping sublimity and beauty with no thought of literary schemes. Yet his every-day talk about his favorite trees and glaciers had more of the glow of poetry in it than any talk I have ever heard from men of letters, and his books and *Journal* will long perpetuate this thrilling sense of personal contact with wild, clean, uplifted things — blossoms in giant tree-tops and snow-eddies blowing round the shoulders of Alaskan peaks. Here is a West as far above Jack London's and Frank Norris's as the snow-line is higher than the jungle.

The rediscovery of the South was not so much an exploration of fresh or forgotten geographical territory, as it was a new perception of the romantic human material offered by a peculiar civilization. Political and social causes had long kept the South in isolation. A few writers like Wirt, Kennedy, Longstreet, Simms, had described various aspects of its life with grace or vivacity, but the best picture of colonial Virginia had been drawn, after all, by Thackeray, who had merely read about it in books. Visitors like Fanny Kemble and

Frederick Law Olmsted sketched the South of the mid-nineteenth century more vividly than did the sons of the soil. There was no real literary public in the South for a native writer like Simms. He was as dependent upon New York and the Northern market as a Virginian tobacco-planter of 1740 had been upon London. But within a dozen years after the close of the War and culminating in the eighteen-nineties, there came a rich and varied harvest of Southern writing, notably in the field of fiction. The public for these stories, it is true, was still largely in the North and West, and it was the magazines and publishing-houses of New York and Boston that gave the Southern authors their chief stimulus and support. It was one of the happy proofs of the solidarity of the new nation.

The romance of the Spanish and French civilization of New Orleans, as revealed in Mr. Cable's fascinating *Old Creole Days*, was recognized, not as something merely provincial in its significance, but as contributing to the infinitely variegated pattern of our national life. Irwin Russell, Joel Chandler Harris, and Thomas Nelson Page portrayed in verse and prose the humorous, pathetic, unique traits of the Southern negro, a type hitherto

GEORGE W. CABLE

Photograph.

BRET HARTE

Photograph.

SIDNEY LANIER

Photograph.

GEORGE W. CABLE
Photograph.

BRET HARTE
Photograph.

SIDNEY LANIER
Photograph.

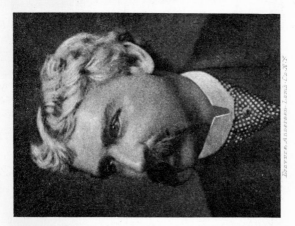

Brown & Anderson Lond. Co. N.Y.

chiefly sketched in caricature or by strangers.
Page, Hopkinson Smith, Grace King, and a score
of other artists began to draw affectionate pictures of the vanished Southern mansion of plantation days, when all the women were beautiful and
all the men were brave, when the very horses were
more spirited and the dogs lazier and the honey-
suckles sweeter and the moonlight more entrancing
than today. Miss Murfree ("C. E. Craddock")
charmed city-dwellers and country-folk alike by
her novels of the Tennessee mountains. James
Lane Allen painted lovingly the hemp-fields and
pastures of Kentucky. American magazines of
the decade from 1880 to 1890 show the complete
triumph of dialect and local color, and this movement, so full of interest to students of the immense
divergence of American types, owed much of its
vitality to the talent of Southern writers.

But the impulse spread far beyond the South.
Early in the seventies Edward Eggleston wrote
The Hoosier Schoolmaster and *The Circuit Rider*,
faithful and moving presentations of genuine pioneer types which were destined to pass with
the frontier settlements. Soon James Whitcomb
Riley was to sing of the next generation of Hoosiers,
who frequented *The Old Swimmin' Hole* and re-

joiced *When the Frost is on the Punkin*. It was the era of Denman Thompson's plays, *Joshua Whitcomb* and *The Old Homestead*. Both the homely and the exotic marched under this banner of local color: Hamlin Garland presented Iowa barnyards and cornfields, Helen Hunt Jackson dreamed the romance of the Mission Indian in *Ramona*, and Lafcadio Hearn, Irish and Greek by blood, resident of New Orleans and not yet an adopted citizen of Japan, tantalized American readers with his *Chinese Ghosts* and *Chita*. A fascinating period it seems, as one looks back upon it, and it lasted until about the end of the century, when the suddenly discovered commercial value of the historical novel and the ensuing competition in best sellers misled many a fine artistic talent and coarsened the public taste. The New South then played the lite.ary market as recklessly as the New West.

Let us glance back to "the abandoned farm of literature," as a witty New Yorker once characterized New England. The last quarter of the nineteenth century witnessed a decline in the direct influence of that province over the country as a whole. Its strength sapped by the emigration of its more vigorous sons, its typical institutions sagging under the weight of immense immigrations from Europe, its political importance growing more and more negligible, that ancient promontory of ideas has continued to lose its relative literary significance. In one field of literature only has New England maintained its rank since the Civil War, and that is in the local short story. Here women have distinguished themselves beyond the proved capacity of New England men. Mrs. Stowe and Rose Terry Cooke, women of democratic humor, were the pioneers; then came Harriet Prescott Spofford and Elizabeth Stuart Phelps, women with nerves; and finally the three artists who have written, out of the material offered by a decadent New England, as perfect short stories as France or Russia can produce—Sarah Orne Jewett, Mary Wilkins Freeman, and Alice Brown. These gifted writers portrayed, with varying technique and with singular differences in their instinctive choice of material, the dominant qualities of an isolated, in-bred race, still proud in its decline; still inquisitive and acquisitive, versatile yet stubborn, with thrift passing over into avarice, and mental power degenerating into smartness; cold and hard under long repression of emotion, yet capable of passion and fanaticism; at worst, a mere trader, a crank, a grim recluse; at best, endowed with an austere physical and moral beauty. Miss Jewett preferred to touch graciously the sunnier slopes of this provincial temperament, to linger in its ancient dignities and serenities. Miss Brown has shown the pathos of its thwarted desires, its hunger for a beauty and a happiness denied. Mary Wilkins Freeman revealed its fundamental tragedies of will.

Two of the best known writers of New England fiction in this period were not natives of the soil, though they surpassed most native New Englanders in their understanding of the type. They were William Dean Howells and Henry James. Mr. Howells, who, in his own words, "can reasonably suppose that it is because of the mixture of Welsh, German, and Irish in me that I feel myself so typically American," came to "the Holy Land at Boston" as a "passionate pilgrim from the West." *A Boy's Town, My Literary Passions*, and *Years of my Youth* make clear the image of the young poet-journalist who returned from his four years in Venice and became assistant editor of *The Atlantic Monthly* in 1866. In 1871 he succeeded Fields in the editorship, but it was not until after his resignation in 1881 that he could put his full strength into those realistic novels of contemporary New England which established his fame as a writer. *A Modern Instance* and *The Rise of Silas Lapham* are perhaps the finest stories of this group; and the latter novel may prove to be Mr. Howells's chief "visiting-card to posterity." We cannot here follow him to New York and to a new phase of novel writing, begun with *A Hazard of New Fortunes*, nor can we discuss the now antiquated debate upon realism which was waged in the eighteen-eighties over the books of Howells and James. We must content ourselves with saying that a knowledge of Mr. Howells's work is essential to the student of the American provincial novel, as it is also to the student of our more generalized types of story-writing, and that he has never in his long career written an insincere, a slovenly, or an infelicitous page. *My Literary Friends and Acquaintance* gives the most charming picture ever drawn of the elder Cambridge, Concord, and Boston men who ruled over our literature when young Howells came out of the West, and *My Mark Twain* is his memorable portrait of another type of sovereign, perhaps the dynasty that will rule the future.

Although Henry James, like Mr. Howells, wrote at one time acute studies of New England character, he was never, in his relations to that section, or, for that matter, to any locality save possibly London, anything more than a "visiting mind." His grandfather was an Irish merchant in Albany. His father, Henry James, was a philosopher and wit, a man of comfortable fortune, who lived at times in Newport, Concord, and Boston, but who was residing in New York when his son Henry was born in 1843. No child was ever made the subject of a more complete theory of deracination. Transplanted from city to city, from country to country, without a family or a voting-place, without college or church or creed or profession or responsibility of any kind save to his own exigent ideals of truth and beauty, Henry James came to be the very pattern of a cosmopolitan. Avoiding his native country for nearly thirty years and then returning for a few months to write some intricate pages about that *American Scene* which he understood far less truly than the average immigrant, he died in 1916 in London, having just renounced his American citizenship and become a British subject in order to show his sympathy with the Empire, then at war. It was the sole evidence of political emotion in a lifetime of seventy-three years.

American writing men are justly proud, nevertheless, of this expatriated craftsman. The American is inclined to admire good workmanship of any kind, as far as he can understand the mechanism of it. The task of really understanding Henry James has been left chiefly to clever women and to a few critics, but ever since *A Passionate Pilgrim* and *Roderick Hudson* appeared in 1875, it has been recognized that here was a master, in his own fashion. What that fashion is may now be known by anyone who will take the pains to read the author's prefaces to the New York edition of his revised works. Never, not even in the Paris which James loved, has an artist put his intentions and his self-criticism more definitively upon paper. The secret of Henry James is told plainly enough here: a specially equipped intelligence, a freedom from normal responsibilities, a consuming desire to create beautiful things, and, as life unfolded its complexities and *nuances* before his vision, an increasing passion to seek the beauty which lies entangled and betrayed, a beauty often adumbrated rather than made plastic, stories that must be hinted at rather than told, raptures that exist for the initiated only. The much discussed early and middle and later manners of James are only various campaigns of this one questing spirit, changing his procedure as the elusive object of his search hid itself by this or that device of protective coloration or swift escape. It is as if a collector of rare butterflies had one method of capturing them in Madagascar, another for the Orinoco, and still another for Japan— though Henry James found his Japan and Orinoco and Madagascar all in London town!

No one who ever had the pleasure of hearing him discourse about the art of fiction can forget the absolute seriousness of his professional devotion; it was as though a shy celebrant were to turn and explain, with mystical intensity and a mystic's involution and reversal of all the values of vulgar speech, the ceremonial of some strange, high altar. His own power as a creative artist was not always commensurate with his intellectual endowment or with his desire after beauty, and his frank contempt for the masses of men made it difficult for him to write English. He preferred, as did Browning, who would have liked to reach the masses, a dialect of his own, and he used it increasingly after he was fifty. It was a dialect capable of infinite gradations of tone, endless refinements of expression. In his threescore books there are delicious poignant moments where the spirit of life itself flutters like a wild creature, half-caught, half-escaping. It is for the beauty and thrill of these moments that the pages of Henry James will continue to be cherished by a few thousand readers scattered throughout the Republic to which he was ever an alien.

No poet of the new era has won the national recognition enjoyed by the veterans. It will be recalled that Bryant survived until 1878, Longfellow and Emerson until 1882, Lowell until 1891, Whittier and Whitman until 1892, and Holmes until 1894. Compared with these men the younger writers of verse seemed overmatched. The *National Ode* for the Centennial celebration in 1876 was intrusted to Bayard Taylor, a hearty person, author of capital books of travel, plentiful verse, and a skilful translation of *Faust*. But an adequate *National Ode* was not in him. Sidney Lanier, who was writing in that year his *Psalm of the West* and was soon to compose *The Marshes of Glynn*, had far more of the divine fire. He was a bookish Georgia youth who had served with the Confederate army, and afterward, with broken health and in dire poverty, gave his brief life to music and poetry. He had rich capacities for both arts, but suffered in both from the lack of discipline and from an impetuous, restless imagination which drove him on to over-ambitious designs. Whatever the flaws in his affluent verse, it has grown constantly in popular favor, and he is, after Poe, the best known poet of the South. The late Edmund Clarence Stedman, whose *American Anthology* and critical articles upon American poets did so much to enhance the reputation of other men, was himself a maker of ringing lyrics and spirited narrative verse. His later days were given increasingly to criticism, and his *Life and Letters* is a storehouse of material bearing upon the growth of New York as a literary market-place during half a century. Richard Watson Gilder was another admirably fine figure, poet, editor, and leader of public opinion in many a noble cause. His *Letters*, likewise, give an intimate picture of literary New York from the seventies to the present. Through his editorship of *Scribner's Monthly* and *The Century Magazine* his sound influence made itself felt upon writers in every section. His own lyric vein had an opaline intensity of fire, but in spite of its glow his verse sometimes refused to sing.

The most perfect poetic craftsman of the period

— and, many think, our one faultless worker in verse — was Thomas Bailey Aldrich. His first volume of juvenile verse had appeared in 1855, the year of Whittier's *Barefoot Boy* and Whitman's *Leaves of Grass*. By 1865 his poems were printed in the then well-known Blue and Gold edition, by Ticknor and Fields. In 1881 he succeeded Howells in the editorship of the *Atlantic*. Aldrich had a versatile talent that turned easily to adroit prose tales, but his heart was in the filing of his verses. Nothing so daintily perfect as his lighter pieces has been produced on this side of the Atlantic, and the deeper notes and occasional darker questionings of his later verse are embodied in lines of impeccable workmanship. Aloof from the social and political conflicts of his day, he gave himself to the fastidious creation of beautiful lines, believing that the beautiful line is the surest road to Arcady, and that Herrick, whom he idolized, had shown the way.

To some readers of these pages it may seem like profanation to pass over poets like Sill, George Woodberry, Edith Thomas, Richard Hovey, William Vaughn Moody, Madison Cawein—to mention but half a dozen distinguished names out of a larger company — and to suggest that James Whitcomb Riley, more completely than any American poet since Longfellow, succeeded in expressing the actual poetic feelings of the men and women who composed his immense audience. Riley, like Aldrich, went to school to Herrick, Keats, Tennyson, and Longfellow, but when he began writing newspaper verse in his native Indiana he was guided by two impulses which gave individuality to his work. "I was always trying to write of the kind of people I knew, and especially to write verse that I could read just as if it were spoken for the first time." The first impulse kept him close to the wholesome Hoosier soil. The second is an anticipation of Robert Frost's theory of speech tones as the basis of verse, as well as a revival of the bardic practice of reciting one's own poems. For Riley had much of the actor and platform-artist in him, and comprehended that poetry might be made again a spoken art, directed to the ear rather than to the eye. His vogue, which at his death in 1915 far surpassed that of any living American poet, is inexplicable to those persons only who forget the sentimental traditions of our American literature and its frank appeal to the emotions of juvenility, actual and recollected. Riley's best "holt" as a poet was his memory of his own boyhood and his perception that the child-mind lingers in every adult reader. Genius has often been called the gift of prolonged adolescence, and in this sense, surely, there was genius in the warm and gentle heart of this fortunate provincial who held that "old Indianapolis" was "high Heaven's sole and only under-study." No one has ever had the audacity to say that of New York.

We have had American drama for one hundred and fifty years,[1] but much of it, like our popular fiction and poetry, has been subliterary, more interesting to the student of social life and national character than to literary criticism in the narrow sense of that term. Few of our best known literary men have written for the stage. The public has preferred melodrama to poetic tragedy, although perhaps the greatest successes have been scored by plays which are comedies of manners rather than melodrama, and character studies of various American types, built up around the known capabilities of a particular actor. The twentieth century has witnessed a marked activity in play-writing, in the technical study of the drama,

[1] *Representative American Plays,* edited by Arthur Hobson Quinn, N. Y., 1917.

and in experiment with dramatic production, particularly with motion pictures and the out-of-doors pageant. At no time since *The Prince of Parthia* was first acted in Philadelphia in 1767 has such a large percentage of Americans been artistically and commercially interested in the drama, but as to the literary results of the new movement it is too soon to speak.

Nor is it possible to forecast the effect of a still more striking movement of contemporary taste, the revival of interest in poetry and the experimentation with new poetical forms. Such revival and experiment have often, in the past, been the preludes of great epochs of poetical production. Living Americans have certainly never seen such a widespread demand for contemporary verse, such technical curiosity as to the possible forms of poetry, or such variety of bold innovation. Imagism itself is hardly as novel as its contemporary advocates appear to maintain, and free verse goes back far in our English speech and song. But the new generation believes that it has made a discovery in reverting to sensations rather than thought, to the naïve reproduction of retinal and muscular impressions, as if this were the end of the matter.

The self-conscious, self-defending side of the new poetic impulse may soon pass, as it did in the case of Wordsworth and of Victor Hugo. Whatever happens, we have already had fresh and exquisite revelations of natural beauty, and, in volumes like *North of Boston* and *A Spoon River Anthology*, judgments of life that run very deep.

American fiction seems just now, on the contrary, to be marking time and not to be getting noticeably forward. Few names unknown ten years ago have won wide recognition in the domain of the novel. The short story has made little technical advance since the first successes of "O. Henry," though the talent of many observers has dealt with new material offered by the racial characteristics of European immigrants and by new phases of commerce and industry. The enormous commercial demand of the five-cent weeklies for short stories of a few easily recognized patterns has resulted too often in a substitution of stencil-plate generalized types instead of delicately and powerfully imagined individual characters. Short stories have been assembled, like Ford cars, with amazing mechanical expertness, but with little artistic advance in design. The same temporary arrest of progress has been noted in France and England, however, where different causes have been at work. No one can tell, in truth, what makes some plants in the literary garden wither at the same moment that others are outgrowing their borders.

There is one plant in our own garden, however, whose flourishing state will be denied by nobody— namely, that kind of nature-writing identified with Thoreau and practised by Thomas Wentworth Higginson, Starr King, John Burroughs, John Muir, Clarence King, Bradford Torrey, Theodore Roosevelt, William J. Long, Thompson-Seton, Stewart Edward White, and many others. Their books represent, Professor Canby[1] believes, the adventures of the American subconsciousness, the promptings of forgotten memories, a racial tradition of contact with the wilderness, and hence one of the most genuinely American traits of our literature.

Other forms of essay writing, surely, have seemed in our own generation less distinctive of our peculiar quality. While admirable biographical and critical studies appear from time to time, and here and there a whimsical or trenchant discursive essay like those of Miss Repplier or Dr.

[1] " Back to Nature," by H. S. Canby, *Yale Review*, July, 1917.

HENRY JAMES

Painting by Blanche, exhibited in the Salon, Paris, 1909.

HENRY JAMES

Painting by Blanche, exhibited in the Salon, Paris, 1909.

Crothers, no one would claim that we approach France or even England in the field of criticism, literary history, memoirs, the bookish essay, and biography. We may have race-memories of a pine-tree which help us to write vigorously and poetically about it, but we write less vitally as soon as we enter the library door. A Frenchman does not, for he is better trained to perceive the continuity and integrity of race-consciousness, in the whole field of its manifestation. He does not feel, as many Americans do, that they are turning their back on life when they turn to books.

Perhaps the truth is that although we are a reading people we are not yet a book-loving people. The American newspaper and magazine have been successful in making their readers fancy that newspaper and magazine are an equivalent for books. Popular orators and popular preachers confirm this impression, and colleges and universities have often emphasized a vocational choice of books — in other words, books that are not books at all, but treatises. It is not, of course, that American journalism, whether of the daily or monthly sort, has consciously set itself to supplant the habit of book-reading. A thousand social and economic factors enter into such a problem. But few observers will question the assertion that the influence of the American magazine, ever since its great period of national literary service in the eighties and nineties, has been more marked in the field of conduct and of artistic taste than in the stimulation of a critical literary judgment. An American schoolhouse of today owes its improvement in appearance over the schoolhouse of fifty years ago largely to the popular diffusion, through the illustrated magazines, of better standards of artistic taste. But whether the judgment of school-teachers and school-children upon a piece of literature is any better than it was in the red schoolhouse of fifty years ago is a disputable question.

But we must stop guessing, or we shall never have done. The fundamental problem of our literature, as this book has attempted to trace it, has been to obtain from a mixed population dwelling in sections as widely separated as the peoples of Northern and Southern Europe, an integral intellectual and spiritual activity which could express, in obedience to the laws of beauty and truth, the emotions stimulated by our national life. It has been assumed in the preceding chapters that

American literature is something different from English literature written in America. Canadian and Australian literatures have indigenous qualities of their own, but typically they belong to the colonial literature of Great Britain. This can scarcely be said of the writings of Franklin and Jefferson, and it certainly cannot be said of the writings of Cooper, Hawthorne, Emerson, Thoreau, Whitman, Lowell, Lincoln, Mark Twain, and Mr. Howells. In the pages of these men and of hundreds of others less distinguished, there is a revelation of a new national type. That the full energies of this nation have been back of our books, giving them a range and vitality and unity commensurate with the national existence, no one would claim. There are other spheres of effort in which American character has been more adequately expressed than in words. Nevertheless the books are here, in spite of every defect in national discipline, every flaw in national character; and they deserve the closest attention from all those who are trying to understand the American mind.

If the effort toward an expression of a peculiarly complex national experience has been the problem of our literary past, the literary problem of the future is the expression of the adjustment of American ideals to the standards of civilization. "Patriotism," said the martyred Edith Cavell just before her death, "is not enough." Nationality and the instincts of national separatism now seem essential to the preservation of the political units of the world-state, precisely as a healthy individualism must be the basis of all enduring social fellowship. Yet it is clear that civilization is a larger, more ultimate term than nationality. Chauvinism is nowhere more repellent than in the things of the mind. It is difficult for some Americans to think internationally even in political affairs — to construe our national policy and duty in terms of obligation to civilization. Nevertheless the task must be faced, and we are slowly realizing it.

In the field of literature, likewise, Americanism is not a final word either of blame or praise. It is a word of useful characterization. Only American books, and not books written in English in America, can adequately represent our national contribution to the world's thinking and feeling. So argued Emerson and Whitman, long ago. But the younger of these two poets came to realize in his old age that the New World and the Old World are fundamentally one. The literature of

the New World will inevitably have an accent of
its own, but it must speak the mother-language of
civilization, share in its culture, accept its discipline.

It has been said disparagingly of Longfellow
and his friends: "The houses of the Brahmins had
only eastern windows. The souls of the whole
school lived in the old lands of culture, and they
visited these lands as often as they could, and,
returning, brought back whole libraries of books
which they eagerly translated." But even if
Longfellow and his friends had been nothing more
than translators and diffusers of European culture,
their task would have been justified. They kept
the ideals of civilization from perishing in this new
soil. Through those eastern windows came in, and
still comes in, the sunlight to illumine the American spirit. To decry the literatures of the Orient and of Greece and Rome as something now
outgrown by America, is simply to close the
eastern windows, to narrow our conception of civilization to merely national and contemporaneous
terms. It is as provincial to attempt this restriction in literature as it would be in world-politics.
We must have all the windows open in our American writing, free access to ideas, knowledge of
universal standards, perception of universal law.

BIBLIOGRAPHICAL NOTE

AN authoritative account of American Literature to
the close of the Revolution is given in M. C. Tyler's
*History of American Literature during the Colonial
Time*, 2 volumes (1878) and *Literary History of the
American Revolution*, 2 volumes (1897). For a general
survey see Barrett Wendell, *A Literary History of
America* (1900), W. P. Trent, *American Literature*
(1903), G. E. Woodberry, *America in Literature*
(1903), W. C. Bronson, *A Short History of American
Literature* (1903), with an excellent bibliography, W. B.
Cairns, *History of American Literature* (1912), W. P.
Trent and J. Erskine, *Great American Writers* (1912),
and W. Riley, *American Thought* (1915). The most
recent and authoritative account is to be found in *The
Cambridge History of American Literature*, 3 volumes
edited by Trent, Erskine, Sherman, and Van Doren.

The best collection of American prose and verse
is E. C. Stedman and E. M. Hutchinson's *Library of American Literature*, 11 volumes (1888–
1890). For verse alone, see E. C. Stedman, *An
American Anthology* (1900), and W. C. Bronson,
American Poems, 1625–1892 (1912). For criticism
of leading authors, note W. C. Brownell, *American
Prose Masters* (1909), and Stedman, *Poets of America*
(1885).

Chapters 1–3. Note W. Bradford, *Journal* (1898), J. Winthrop, *Journal* (1825, 1826), also *Life and Letters* by R. C. Winthrop, 2 volumes (1863), G. L. Walker, *Thomas Hooker* (1891), O. S. Straus, *Roger Williams* (1894), Cotton Mather, *Diary,* 2 volumes (1911, 1912), also his *Life* by Barrett Wendell (1891), Samuel Sewall, *Diary,* 3 volumes (1878). For Jonathan Edwards, see *Works,* 4 volumes (1852), his *Life* by A. V. G. Allen (1889), *Selected Sermons* edited by H. N. Gardiner (1904). The most recent edition of Franklin's *Works* is edited by A. H. Smyth, 10 volumes (1907).

Chapter 4. Samuel Adams, *Works,* 4 volumes (1904), John Adams, *Works,* 10 volumes (1856), Thomas Paine, *Life* by M. D. Conway, 2 volumes (1892), *Works* edited by Conway, 4 volumes (1895), Philip Freneau, *Poems,* 3 volumes (Princeton edition, 1902), Thomas Jefferson, *Works* edited by P. L. Ford, 10 volumes (1892–1898), J. Woolman, *Journal* (edited by Whittier, 1871, and also in *Everyman's Library*), *The Federalist* (edited by H. C. Lodge, 1888).

Chapter 5. Washington Irving, *Works,* 40 volumes (1891–1897), also his *Life and Letters* by P. M. Irving, 4 volumes (1862–1864). Fenimore Cooper, *Works,* 32 volumes (1896), *Life* by T. R. Lounsbury (1883). Brockden Brown, *Works,* 6 volumes, (1887). W. C. Bryant, *Poems,* 2 volumes (1883), *Prose,* 2 volumes (1884), and his *Life* by John Bigelow (1890).

Chapter 6. H. C. Goddard, *Studies in New England Transcendentalism* (1908). R. W. Emerson, *Works,* 12 volumes (Centenary edition, 1903), *Journal*, 10 volumes (1909–1914), his *Life* by J. E. Cabot, 2 volumes (1887), by R. Garnett (1887), by G. E. Woodberry (1905); see also *Ralph Waldo Emerson*, a critical study by O. W. Firkins (1915). H. D. Thoreau, *Works*, 20 volumes (Walden edition including *Journals*, 1906), *Life* by F. B. Sanborn (1917), also *Thoreau, A Critical Study* by Mark van Doren (1916). Note also Lindsay Swift, *Brook Farm* (1900), and *The Dial*, reprint by the Rowfant Club (1902).

Chapter 7. Hawthorne, *Works*, 12 volumes (1882), *Life* by G. E. Woodberry (1902). Longfellow, *Works*, 11 volumes (1886), *Life* by Samuel Longfellow, 3 volumes (1891). Whittier, *Works*, 7 volumes (1892), *Life* by S. T. Pickard, 2 volumes (1894). Holmes, *Works*, 13 volumes (1892), *Life* by J. T. Morse, Jr. (1896). Lowell, *Works*, 11 volumes (1890), *Life* by Ferris Greenslet (1905), *Letters* edited by C. E. Norton, 2 volumes (1893). For the historians, note H. B. Adams, *Life and Writings of Jared Sparks*, 2 volumes (1893). M. A. DeW. Howe, *Life and Letters of George Bancroft*, 2 volumes (1908), G. S. Hillard, *Life, Letters, and Journals of George Ticknor*, 2 volumes (1876), George Ticknor, *Life of Prescott* (1863), also Rollo Ogden, *Life of Prescott* (1904), G. W. Curtis, *Correspondence of J. L. Motley*, 2 volumes (1889), Francis Parkman, *Works*, 12 volumes (1865–1898), *Life* by C. H. Farnham (1900), J. F. Jameson, *History of Historical Writing in America* (1891).

Chapter 8. Poe, *Works*, 10 volumes (Stedman-Woodberry edition, 1894–1895), also 17 volumes (Virginia edition, J. A. Harrison, 1902), *Life* by G. E. Woodberry, 2 volumes (1909). Whitman, *Leaves of Grass* and *Complete Prose Works* (Small, Maynard and Co.) (1897, 1898), also John Burroughs, *A Study of Whitman* (1896).

Chapter 9. C. Schurz, *Life of Henry Clay*, 2 volumes (1887). Daniel Webster, *Works*, 6 volumes (1851), *Life* by H. C. Lodge (1883). Rufus Choate, *Works*, 2 volumes (1862). Wendell Phillips, *Speeches, Lectures, and Letters*, 2 volumes (1892). W. L. Garrison, *The Story of his Life Told by his Children*, 4 volumes (1885–1889). Harriet Beecher Stowe, *Works*, 17 volumes (1897), *Life* by C. E. Stowe (1889). Abraham Lincoln, *Works*, 2 volumes (edited by Nicolay and Hay, 1894).

Chapter 10. For an excellent bibliography of the New National Period, see F. L. Pattee, *A History of American Literature since 1870* (1916).

For further bibliographical information the reader is referred to the articles on American authors in *The Encyclopædia Britannica* and in *The Warner Library* (volume 30, *The Student's Course*, N. Y., 1917).

INDEX

Adams, C. F., 7

Adams, John, opinion of American independence, 11–12; as a writer, 73

Adams, Samuel, 73–74, 209

After the Burial, Lowell, 172

Agassiz, Fiftieth Birthday of, Longfellow, 156

Age of Reason, Paine, 75

Ages, The, Bryant, 104

Alcott, Bronson, 118, 119, 139–140

Aldrich, T. B., 256–57

Alhambra, The, Irving, 91

Allen, J. L., 247

American Anthology, Stedman, 256

American characteristics, 3–5

American colonies, literature in the 17th century, 25–42; journalism, 60–62; education, 62–63; science, 63–64; bibliography of the literature, 269–270

American colonists, predominantly English, 12–25; motives for emigration, 16; moulded by pioneer life, 17–23; in 1760, 59–60

"American idea," 206–07

American life since the Civil War, 234 *et seq.*

American literature, the term, 6

American Mercury, 61

American Scholar, The, Emerson, 123

Ames, Fisher, 88

Among my Books, Lowell, 170

Andrew Rykman's Prayer, Whittier, 161

Annabel Lee, Poe, 192

Anthologies, American, 269

Arsenal at Springfield, The, Longfellow, 156

Assignation, The, Poe, 193

Astoria, Irving, 91

Atala, Châteaubriand, 96

Atlantic Monthly, 161, 167, 170, 250, 257

Autobiography, Franklin, 58–59

Autocrat of the Breakfast Table, The, Holmes, 164, 167

Bacchus, Emerson, 129

Ballad of the French Fleet, A, Longfellow, 155

Bancroft, George, 89, 176, 177–78

Barefoot Boy, The, Whittier, 158

Bartol, C. A., 115

Battle Hymn of the Republic, Howe, 224, 225

Battle of the Kegs, The, Hopkinson, 69

Bay Psalm Book, 35

Beecher, H. W., 216–17

Belfry of Bruges, The, Longfellow, 156

Bells, The, Poe, 5–6, 192

Biglow Papers, The, Lowell, 170, 172, 173

Black Cat, The, Poe, 194

Blaine, J. G., quoted, 163

Blithedale Romance, The, Hawthorne, 145–46, 150–51

280   **INDEX**